Humanitarian Ecological Economics and Accounting

The strict conversation of financial capital allows accountants to preserve capitalism in its current form. Thus, building a more humane economy will require a new accounting model.

Humanitarian Ecological Economics and Accounting: Capitalism, Ecology and Democracy argues for the adoption of a CARE model: comprehensive accounting in respect of ecology. This new model will take the traditional weapons of capitalist accounting and turn them against capitalism, with a goal to protect and conserve human and natural capital within the framework of a democratic society. The CARE model has been conceived as the potential basis of a new type of market economy and of a new type of governance of firms and nations. Additionally, this allows for a new conception of capital, cost and profit that helps with moves towards a society of the commons. The first part of the book explores the reconstruction of accounting and economics from the ground up, outlining the theoretical basis for the model. The second part of the book explores the transformation of the governance of firms and nations. Finally, an additional section is dedicated to the conception of a new model of national accounting.

This book will be of significant interest to readers of ecological economics, critical accounting and heterodox economics.

Jacques Richard is Emeritus Professor at the University of Paris Dauphine, France. He is also an ex chartered Accountant and Counsellor of Trade Unions, and ex Member of the Authority of Accounting Standards (Paris). In 2013 he received the 'Best Manuscript Award' from the Academy of Accounting Historians.

Alexandre Rambaud is Doctor of Mathematics and Management Sciences, and *maître de conférences* at AgroParisTech – CIRED. He is also Associate Researcher at the University of Paris Dauphine, France, and co-head of the *Chaire Comptabilité Ecologique*.

Economics and Humanities

Series Editor: Sebastian Berger

University of the West of England (UWE Bristol), UK

The *Economics and Humanities* series presents the economic wisdom of the humanities and arts. Its volumes gather the economic senses sheltered and revealed by some of the most excellent sources within philosophy, poetry, art, and story-telling. By re-rooting economics in its original domain these contributions allow economic phenomena and their meanings to come into the open more fully; indeed, they allow us to ask anew the question "What is economics?". Economic truth is thus shown to arise from the Human rather than the Market.

Readers will gain a foundational understanding of a humanities-based economics and find their economic sensibility enriched. They should turn to this series if they are interested in questions such as: What are the economic consequences of rooting economic Truth in the Human? What is the purpose of a humanities-based economics? What is the proper meaning of the "oikos", and how does it arise? What are the true meanings of wealth and poverty, gain and loss, capital and productivity? In what sense is economic reasoning with words more fundamental than reasoning with numbers? What is the dimension and measure of human dwelling in the material world?

These volumes address themselves to all those who are interested in sources and foundations for economic wisdom. Students and academics who are fundamentally dissatisfied with the state of economics and worried that its crisis undermines society will find this series of interest.

Economics, Accounting and the True Nature of Capitalism
Capitalism, Ecology and Democracy
Jacques Richard and Alexandre Rambaud

Humanitarian Ecological Economics and Accounting
Capitalism, Ecology and Democracy
Jacques Richard and Alexandre Rambaud

For more information about this series, please visit: www.routledge.com/ Economics-and-Humanities/book-series/RSECH

Humanitarian Ecological Economics and Accounting

Capitalism, Ecology and Democracy

Jacques Richard and Alexandre Rambaud

Routledge
Taylor & Francis Group

LONDON AND NEW YORK

First published 2022
by Routledge
2 Park Square, Milton Park, Abingdon, Oxon OX14 4RN

and by Routledge
605 Third Avenue, New York, NY 10158

Routledge is an imprint of the Taylor & Francis Group, an informa business

British Library Cataloguing-in-Publication Data
A catalogue record for this book is available from the British Library

Library of Congress Cataloging-in-Publication Data
Names: Richard, Jacques, author. | Rambaud, Alexandre, author.
Title: Humanitarian ecological economics and accounting : capitalism, ecology and democracy / Jacques Richard and Alexandre Rambaud.
Description: Milton Park, Abingdon, Oxon ; New York, NY : Routledge, 2022. | Series: Economics and humanities | Includes bibliographical references and index.
Identifiers: LCCN 2021027865 (print) | LCCN 2021027866 (ebook) | ISBN 9781032046617 (hardback) | ISBN 9781032046648 (paperback) | ISBN 9781003194149 (ebook)
Subjects: LCSH: Environmental economics. | Capitalism. | Ecology—Economic aspects.
Classification: LCC HC79.E5 R514 2022 (print) | LCC HC79.E5 (ebook) | DDC 333.7—dc23
LC record available at https://lccn.loc.gov/2021027865
LC ebook record available at https://lccn.loc.gov/2021027866

ISBN: 978-1-032-04661-7 (hbk)
ISBN: 978-1-032-04664-8 (pbk)
ISBN: 978-1-003-19414-9 (ebk)

DOI: 10.4324/9781003194149

Typeset in Times New Roman
by Apex CoVantage, LLC

Contents

Introduction

In a previous volume dedicated to the reconceptualization of the notion of capitalism we have shown that the capitalist system is entirely dominated by pernicious accounting laws and practices. Without their destruction and replacement there will hardly be chance to form a new ecological and humane society. The issue of socialists and communists is that they have never wanted or been able to conceive a true and credible alternative to the capitalist system. At best, the former only made it more sustainable without suppressing it. The latter deceived themselves with authoritarian models directed against private property and markets: their Marxist philosophy and actions have revealed to be even worse than capitalism. Thus, today as Ogilvie (2012, 49) says, "we are very far away from seeing a weapon against liberalism and its market economy". What we need is a means to achieve a true accounting revolution. An ecological and human accounting revolution against the financial revolution (Beaver, 1989). This is why we propose a new accounting model whose goal will be to protect human and natural capitals in the frame of a democratic society with markets.[1] This model is the CARE/TDL model (CARE: "Comprehensive Accounting in Respect of Ecology". TDL: "Triple Depreciation Line"). It has been conceived in order to be the basis of a new type of market economy and a new governance of firms and nations. This volume comprises two main parts. The first will be devoted to the reconstruction of accounting and economics, and the second to a proposal for a new governance of firms and nations.

Note

1 We will use for that preceding works, notably Richard 2012a, Rambaud, 2015; Rambaud and Richard, 2015a, 2015b, 2016, 2017, 2018; Richard and Rambaud, 2020.

DOI: 10.4324/9781003194149-1

Part I

The reconstruction of accounting and economics

Introduction

Contrary to the case of Aristotle[1] and his followers our main problem in this book is not to hold forth upon the supreme good or happiness of a part of mankind, but to deal with the *conservation* of all mankind and its ability to govern itself as autonomous persons. And this is not a simple task. As the saying goes it is easy to criticize something, yet much more difficult to propose another thing to replace it. This can be applied to the case of the capitalist economy. The capitalist system has proved to be able to produce wealth. But it has been at the expense of the persistence of a considerable inequality of people (Alvaredo et al., 2018), of its incapacity to give to the workers in the firms a possibility to have a real say on their fate, and of a dramatic destruction of nature (Bonneuil and Fressoz, 2013; Lewis and Maslin, 2015; Moore, 2017).Concerning the last point, Bonneuil and Fressoz assert that we have entered a new period of "Anthropocene". But it will be more convenient to speak of "Capitalocene" as the economic system which is responsible for today's situation since the 13th century is the (modern) capitalist system.[2] To remedy this situation it is easy to formulate such pretty phrases like "we are against the dictatorship of numbers", or, "we must treat other people as an end not as a means[3]" or, again, "humanism and naturalism are not contradictory". All these beautiful sentences, alas, give us no concrete solution to change the capitalist economic system and replace it with a new economic system. As proven by the dramatic warning of a group of concerned scientists[4] the time has gone for a *radical* change of our economic system. Unfortunately many philosophers and politicians, and even economists, have little if not nothing to propose to replace the capitalist *management*. For example, the philosopher Mouffe (2007, 76) regrets that, since the fall of socialism, there is no longer any socialist theory of *management*, but she does not give any concrete proposal to remedy to this vacuum. All the more than her belief is that "any order is necessary

DOI: 10.4324/9781003194149-2

hegemonic" (139). Rorty (1991) only deems that politics is an affair of compromises. More dangerously Comte-Sponville (2004, 72) thinks that capitalism is amoral (not moral or immoral) and that its economic order belongs
to the scientific field of knowledge[5] which imply that its economic rules are
to be accepted as rational ones. Fortunately, Renouard (2013, 40)
contests this view.[6] As far as Giddens (1999, 39) is concerned he does not
go further than Comte-Sponville because he thinks that we have to content
ourselves with capitalism. Deleuze and Guattari (1972) go much further:
they dare to suggest that the solution to the problems lies in the very development of capitalism (as we discuss later in this chapter).Other philosophers like Helmer (2013), inspired by Epicurian views, propose that we
make an individual cure of wisdom based on aponia and ataraxia. But such
remedies, counselled at least since 300 BC, have not permitted to change
the capitalist world, and if we had to choose a philosophy we will thus prefer the stoic sense of duty than the Epicurean serenity. As far as the politicians are concerned, most socialists, such as Blair, Mitterand and Hollande,
have followed the strategy of the compromise with capitalism, which will
conduct their party to catastrophe. Similarly, a majority of economists only
propose ineffective tools inspired by the neoclassical school (more on this
later in this chapter).We think that to concretely fight the capitalist system
one must go beyond the simple sayings or individual spiritualism or compromises. To do that one must first know the capitalist accounting which is
at the heart of this terrible economic system and propose something to
replace it. Our thesis is that the majority of today's economists are not in a
position to propose a real and effective solution to replace capitalism
because they do not know its accounting theory and practice. Only very few
of them like Kapp (1950) and Passet (1979), and their followers like Berger
(2017), underline the fundamental role of accounting to take account of the
social and environmental costs. The task of destruction-reconstruction of
the capitalist system is all the more difficult because, to complicate the situation, the rare concrete preceding attempts to defeat it have dramatically
failed. It is chiefly the case of the Soviet and Maoist experiences, but also,
to a lesser degree, of the Yugoslavian experience, albeit marked by some
interesting aspects. Even the social and solidarity economy and the movement of the Commons initiated by Ostrom (1990) have been obliged to
make compromises with the capitalist economy: they do not represent a real
menace for it, notably for a lack of true alternate accounting and management systems. As said by Passet (in Merlant et al., 2003, 11), the politicians
have been unable to give "the slightest sketch of confrontation between
projects of society". The ability of the capitalist system to impose its
accounting model as the sole possibility is impressive. As we have shown
before in Volume 1 of this work, Marx has been unable to propose another

model of accounting adapted to the worker cooperatives. Engels also, in spite of his knowledge of accounting, has not proposed anything in that sense. In his last writing about Dühring (1880) he never speaks about the possibility of a government of worker cooperatives with a specific type of accounting. He traditionally only proposes that the proletariat should transform the means of production into state property[7] (1880, 71). In the case of the Soviet economy it is fascinating to see that, as it has been demonstrated (Richard, 1980, 1983), its leaders, whether Lenin, Stalin or their followers, have been unable to get out of the claws of a kind of capitalist accounting. The monetary double entry accounting system of the ex USSR (see Richard, 1980; on the basis of Makarov, 1966) had conserved a balance sheet which showed only the financial capital on the liabilities' side. Thus, the only type of capital to be conserved was the capital invested by The Soviet State and managed by a very mighty class of bureaucrats. It has a P&L statement in which the wages of the salaried workers appeared as *expenses diminishing the profit of the bureaucrats.* Although (or may be because) it has been presented as based on "Marxism" and "dialectical materialism" (Makarov, 1966, 3 and 4), it had "singed" the private capitalism. It had been, as said by numerous commentators like Rühle (1932), Bettelheim (1974) and Cliff (1955) a "state capitalism". In this accounting system the accounting profit was that of the "Nomenklatura". It corresponded to the Marxian surplus value available after payment of the wages of the employees. This profit, in an additive formulation, to use private capitalist accounting words, was the sum of three elements: the interests (paid to the Gosbank), the taxes (collected by central state organizations) and the pure profit of the state firms. This system was directed by a class of managers of public enterprises much more powerful than their counterpart of private enterprises in the West. One can say that it was the complete realization of the managerial power of which Say, Saint Simon, Comte, and Berle and Means have dreamt. From the point of view of democracy and of the economy this system was worse than the capitalist system, but very comparable from the point of view of the accounting tools. Lenin, at many times, had repeated that it was necessary to apply the accounting system of the big capitalist firms to increase the productivity of the Soviet labours (Makarov, 1966, 5). A very similar situation existed in Maoist China. The work of Makarov, translated to Chinese, had inspired some accounting books like that one of Zhao, Y., Lou, E., Ge, J., Wu, C. (1979 [1962]). Hence, the same accounting system had appeared in both "socialist" countries. To hide reality, the communist accountants had simply avoided the use of the word capital: Kapital in Russian and Zi Ben (资本) in Chinese. In order to make a formal distinction with the capitalist system of the West they had preferred to use the term "statutory fund" (Ustavni Fond in Russian) and ZI Jin (资金, in Chinese). But this did not change anything of their capitalist philosophy of accounting.[8] It is not surprising that after the collapse of the Soviet Union and the disappearance of Mao these two communist countries have been able to adopt the IFRS and the capitalist market economy of the West without great difficulties. The one experience that could have caused some difficulties to the capitalist system was that of the Self-Management developed at the time of Tito in Yugoslavia (Samary, 2017). In the years 1960–70 the economist Kardelj, helped by innovative accountants, had conceived an original type of accounting adapted to the self-management ideology (Richard, 1983; relying on Jezdimirovic, 1974). It was also a monetary double entry accounting which acts in the frame of a market economy. The original point, in comparison with the Soviet case, was the fact that the employees, theoretically, became "self-managers" and had the right to share between themselves the residual profit. This profit appeared in the P&L statement as the difference between the revenues (sales) and the expenses represented by the consumption of raw materials and services, depreciation expenses, taxes and interest to the banks. In contrast to the capitalist system, there were *no expenses for wages in this accounting system*: the employees got the entire redefined profit and were no longer wage labourers but masters of decisions, notably of the decision concerning the new kind of profit, which became the main source of their day-to-day remuneration. To sum up, they had theoretically totally replaced the shareholders in matters of decisions concerning management, including that of profit. But there were many problems that have complicated this self-management approach. This experience has finally failed for complex reasons of political order (permanent conflicts of diverse nations forced to "cooperate" together under the direction of the communist party; no real possibility of choice other than Tito's regime), geographical reasons (very isolated experience in a small country), economic reasons (state or managerial control of important banks; no system to promote the participation of small private investors to the financing of the firms; competition with capitalist countries which did not have the same constraints) and social reasons (no systematic protection of the human capital on the liabilities side of the balance sheet to the difference of the financial capital[9]). The fact that a kind of social property had been promoted after 1976 has not prevented this country from collapse may be on the contrary. All these experiences and failures belong to the past. They conserve their interest because lessons can be learnt from the information provided, notably on the mistakes that should be avoided in considering a new economic system capable of coping with capitalism. We can distinguish three main lessons. Firstly, the monetary double entry accounting seems to be indispensable: even the revolutionaries of Yugoslavia who wanted to get rid of both capitalism and Leninism or Stalinism maintained this type of accounting. Secondly, it appears that, in any case, a new economic system implies a specific accounting system with a redefinition of the concepts of capital and profit adapted to the new masters in power: it is not a mere question of opening the capitalist books as proposed by Lenin. Perhaps one of the most difficult problems of the social and solidarity economy and of the movement of governing the Commons, which are today interesting experiences, will be to conceive also specific concepts of capital, profit and governance adapted to their ideology[10] to resist to some deviances, notably the quest for power and the indifference to ecological problems (Frémeaux, 2011, 156; Laville, 2010, 346[11]). Indeed, it is very difficult to subsist in a world of systematic price dumping: this is the reason why the capitalists themselves have decided to *impose* a systematic standardization of their accounting system.[12] Thirdly, these experiences show the big dangers resulting from a managerialist conception of the economy as was the case in the former Soviet Union. In conclusion of this (too) short analysis we can assert that today the capitalist system can still "sleep" relatively quietly because it has practically no serious opponent as far as its model of accounting is concerned. It is precisely this challenge that we want to undertake by proposing a new model of accounting for an alternative to capitalism, in spite of today's dominant opinion that capitalism is unavoidable[13] or the best possible solution. In this respect, contrary to the Marxist vulgate, we are not obliged to wait for the maturing of the capitalist system and even the change of the economic basis. As Clastres (1974, 172) has demonstrated with his comparative study of diverse old societies, "it is the political cut which is decisive, not the economic change" so that "the infrastructure is the politics and the super structure the economics". This view is also shared by Castoriadis (1975, 186). In another formulation Victor Hugo has said that "nothing is more powerful than an idea which time has brought". To rebuild capitalist accounting our suggestion is to start from the double entry system imagined at the end of the Middle Ages by merchants such as Datini. The capitalist system which has appeared at that time has not been conceived on the basis of experimental tests of effectiveness.[14] It has been created on the basis of an idea of accounting constraints imposed by the capitalists onto themselves to protect only their financial capital. Our own idea is to broaden this constraint to two other types of capitals with a new accounting system at the service of ecological and human causes. Like some certain martial arts such as Heikido use the force of the adversary and return it against itself! The goal is not to fight against the reason, as proposed by philosophers like Mouffe (2007, 9), but against the unreasonable reason of capitalism. Thus, contrary to Datini, who treated only financial capital as a debt to be reimbursed, we will treat the other two types of capitals in the same way. Accountants are specialists in the conservation of financial capital. It is time that we use their knowledge to the service of mankind. We will then be able not only to redefine the concept of capital but, also, at the same time, the concepts of cost and profit. To conceive and realize this objective we firstly enumerate 12 proposals (or axioms) which will form the basis of the CARE/TDL model: they will be the corner stone of our new model of market economy and the basis of new instrumental norms. Then, secondly, we will compare and contrast this new model of accounting to other proposals of reforms that are nowadays made by the defenders of capitalism. We will show that under the pretension to solve today's ecological and human crisis they are in reality destined to perpetuate the domination of financial capital. This first part will end with a last chapter devoted to an illustration of the application of the CARE/TDL method in micro-economics and macro-economics with the goal to replace the IFRS and the famous GDP; they are both obsolete and dangerous (Richard, 2017).

Notes

1 Hadot (1995, 128–130) underlines that Aristotle considered the (theoretical) search of knowledge for itself as the supreme good; it means a *happy life* free of all material problems, thanks to the activity of the slaves.
2 In the same sense Ferdinand (2019).
3 We refer for the last sentence to Kant who also says, "one's behavior should accord with universalizable maxims which respect persons as ends in themselves".
4 Le Monde (21 fev 2020, 22): "Face to the ecologic crisis the rebellion is necessary" (Our translation).
5 According to him, the capitalist accounting refers to the order of mathematics not of social sciences!
6 She also underlines that Caroll (1991), a theoretician of business ethics famous for their "Pyramid", has also the same erroneous conception of the economics as a neutral field of knowledge (2013, 40).
7 He erroneously believes that there is a progressive appropriation of the means of production by the State (preceded by the Joint Stock Companies) so that the bourgeois (capitalists) have become useless (1880, 69). This will inspire Lenin and his conception of a kind of state capitalism under workers' control. The focus of these fathers of the real socialism is always on questions of property, not on questions of a new type of accounting adapted to socialism.
8 The equation Assets = liabilities was of a classic style (model 1) with the terms "usage of funds = source of funds" (资金fl用=资金来源, zi jin yun yong = zi jin lai yuan).
9 This absence of a systematic protection of human capital has fostered the competition between the workers of the different firms and nations of the Federation, and the appearance of situations of social dumping.
10 Ostrom (1990) has well shown the necessity to have clear rules of governance for the conservation the Commons' resources, but she has not proposed any general concrete solution for that, at least in the field of management.

11 Laville speaks of the danger of institutional isomorphism with the capitalist system which menaces the solidarity economy.
12 Frémeaux (2011, 157), well aware of the problem, logically wants rules to oblige all actors of the economic game to have a sustainable economy.
13 For example Deleuze and Guattari (1972) deem that "capitalism is present in any form of society . . . it is a universal truth".
14 These types of tests are very fashionable today as shown by the reward of Esther Duflo with the Nobel Prize of economics in 2019. It seems to us that the struggle against the poverty must be treated in the same way as the struggle of the capitalists for the conservation of their capital: with strict accounting regulations of conservation determined in democratic ways.

1 Presentation of the 12 basic proposals for the new CARE/TDL accounting model[1]

Introduction

To reconstruct the accounting system we need both a teleology (an ensemble of goals) and axioms (or proposals) which permit to satisfy this teleology. This primacy of goals, notably the fundamental requirements of human life, is a common point with Kapp's philosophy of economics (Berger and Forstater, 2007, 543[2]). Our teleology aims before all at the preservation of the earth and the biosphere (including humanity) which are the basis of any economic system. This is represented by Figure 1.1, conceived by Jacques Weber.

In Figure 1.1 we can see the big horizontal line representing the earth, then the vertical line representing the biosphere (the trunk of life), then a smaller horizontal line representing the human branch and, finally, above this branch, the economy depending of the three preceding elements. If the economy is too "heavy" the whole system can be threatened and there is a

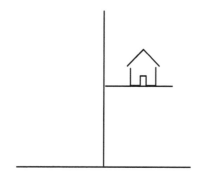

Figure 1.1 The Economy is too heavy for the ecosphere (J Weber)

DOI: 10.4324/9781003194149-3

risk of a collapse: it is the Anthropocene (Lewis and Maslin, 2015) or, better, as we have said before, the Capitalocene. Another representation of this complex and integrated system has been proposed by Passet (1979) with three concentric circles (Richard and Plot, 2014). It is also a convenient representation in line with our philosophy of the question.[3] Thus, we believe that the economic problems before all are questions of values in the sense of ends or teleology. Contrary to Simmel (1918a and 1918b), Tönnies (1923) and, above all, Heidegger (1977), notably to their analysis of the "being toward death", we think that mankind needs some fundamental means and ends toward life; thus we need new accounting for life as opposed to the terrible capitalist accounting which only keeps dead things, like the financial capital. Now, in order to realize this teleology, which has nothing to do with a predestination, we will state the 12 following axioms or proposals.

1–1 First axiom: definition of the concept of capital

As said by Castoriadis (1999, 3) "the very definition of the capital concept and its evolution is not a technical or an economic problem: it reflects a cosmology, an imaginary". We will intend by capital a "thing" material or not, offering a potentiality of usage, and *recognized as to be preserved* for a certain period of time first determined. This definition implies that all the categories which will constitute a (true) capital will be considered as debts corresponding to the systematic conservation of something. We underline that this has nothing to do with the capital concept of mainstream economic literature, which means capital assets or resources to be used. In our conception, on the contrary, it is *not a question of instrumental rationality*. Expressed in more philosophical terms the capital here is an end in itself, not a simple means. The immediate consequence of this definition is that it is impossible to compensate the existence of the different types of capitals, for example to permit the destruction of one of them by the growth of another. To use the vocabulary of ecological economics, the CARE/TDL method relies on a *true* strong sustainability approach and not on a weak one (see Neumayer, 1999 on these concepts). In the frame of this strong sustainability approach it will not be permitted, as it is the case of the conception adopted by the World Bank (2006), to give a global value to the "Wealth of Nations" and to compensate the different financial, human and natural capitals (Richard, 2012). We specify that this approach of a strong sustainability is, as a matter of principle, a strict one. It means that, except for specific cases duly mentioned, it is also not possible to operate compensation inside the different elements composing one broad category of capital.[4] This is obvious for the case of human capital. We cannot imagine in the frame of our philosophy, as it is for example the case of the classical types of national accounting today (see further in this chapter), that the exorbitant revenues of managers like Ghosn (ex-famous PDG of Renault), could compensate the miserable revenues of the French "Yellow vests". This strict rule also applies to the different categories of capitals which compose natural capital. One cannot destruct fish by invoking, as a matter of compensation, the rise of the number of pigs: the problem is maintaining the biosphere; more precisely maintaining its global functioning (see further in this chapter). On the contrary, in the case of financial capital, the principle of no compensation is the exception rather than the rule. For example, the replacement of claims on money by money is not a problem. More largely, the changes in the modes of consumption will cause constant modifications to the types of assets corresponding to the financial capital as a whole.

1–2 Second axiom: the choice of the capitals

It is the task of a democratic society to determine the type of things that deserve to be treated as true capitals. We have seen how capitalists have succeeded, until today, in imposing that the only type of capital to be strictly conserved is their financial stake: this means that only this type of investment has been promoted to the status of a true capital. For us this economic and political choice is at the same time immoral, iniquitous and anti-economic. To change this situation, we propose that *at least* three types of investments (or stakes) into a firm should be treated as (true) capitals: natural, human and financial investments. This normative attitude is based on an ethical categorical imperative, more largely a question of values or ideals.[5] We give more details afterwards on the definition and the characteristics of these three types of capitals. We only indicate that human capital comprises, in a larger sense, the social, societal and artistic capitals. We specify that natural capital must be understood as things (living or not) without which the possibility of life of human beings on the earth would be impossible or, at least, endangered. We admit that it is an anthropocentric view of the question. But, as the philosopher Norton (1991) has demonstrated, it is perfectly possible to conciliate this type of position with the requirements of a systematic preservation or conservation of natural capital (we will not fight a battle on these terms here). We underline that our enumeration of these three capitals is not exhaustive. It is for the citizens to determinate what they consider as other types of capitals: thus, obviously, a tree venerated by an Amazonian tribe can be a capital. Finally, we may conclude on this point that the determination of the list of the capitals refers to a question of axiology[6] and deals with the *most important* question of humanity: what do we want to conserve? Unfortunately, this fundamental ethical question has never really been discussed in the frame of the capitalist- liberal-socialist society. As said by Méda (2013, 172) it is time to re-embed the economy into the ethical realm.

1–3 Third axiom: the necessity of ontological studies

In the case of financial capital we have seen (in Volume 1) that the nature of this capital, in classical accounting, is money invested and due to capitalists. The ontological question here is relatively simple: it offers no significant difficulty, *except in the case of inflation which raises specific problems.* Things are more complicated in the case of natural and human capitals. For these types of capitals, it is impossible to assure their true conservation without thorough and complex ontological studies. These studies will aim to identify the nature of these capitals and the limits of their use.[7]The task is to understand what they really are and how they function in the frame of the global reproduction of the ecosphere and the biosphere (Griffon and Weber, 1996, 174). This approach of the question is at odds with mainstream economic and accounting analyses which talk of so called "human and environmental resources": these types of approaches, in a capitalist way, consider the human and natural capitals only from the point of view of the services (profits) that they can give to capitalists. Our conception of the capital in the CARE/TDL model has notably nothing to do with the measure of "goodwill" associated with the exploitation of nature and humans, and registered on the asset's side of the balance sheet by mainstream economists and accountants (see further in this chapter). Contrary to these capitalist views, the principle of the CARE/TDL method is to systematically preserve nature and humans and, after this preservation, eventually, make a profit, not at a predetermined rate (the famous cost of capital). To sum up, our philosophy is: conserve or preserve to create value and not create value to, eventually, conserve or preserve.[8] In matters of human capital, the goal is to consider the employees as true human beings and give them the possibility to have fulfilled life owing to the social condition of the time, *including the participation in the affairs of their firms* as autonomous persons. It is not to treat them as mere workers destined to give profits to a firm which borrows their services on a labour market. If we accept this type of reasoning which makes of human beings and nature true capitals to be maintained per se and not simple economic means, the question is then, notably, to know in what cases and conditions the *resilience* of these capitals could be endangered. For natural capital, we are obliged to have recourse to the type of studies developed by the literature on the concept of ecological resilience[9] (see, notably, Holling, 1973; Walker et al., 2004; Johnson, 2013). But we can also speak of questions of human resilience when the working conditions of the employees put at stake (threaten) their health and more largely prevent them from having a "good" life[10] (see later in this chapter for this expression). These complex tasks will be carried out by different persons. Firstly, in the case of human capital, this will be undertaken by independent scientists such as ergonomists, occupational therapists, members of trade unions (ASO) with the participation of the concerned persons themselves. In the case of natural capital it will be chiefly done by ecologists, but also by members of NGOs, local residents or members of the firms who have a good knowledge of the specific ecological problems which confront the firms. All these persons will be the *spokeswomen (men)* of nature. The verification of the conservation of these two kinds of capitals will have to be assured by specific auditors in the same way as is provided by financial auditors for financial capital. It would be preferable, however, that, contrary to today's case, these auditors, including financial auditors, will be financed by independent authorities and not by the firms themselves.

1–4 Fourth axiom: the necessity of human and ecological scientific norms and standards

Thanks to the ontological analysis of human and natural capital and their actual state, it will be possible to determine the conditions of their resilience and to deduct on their basis some norms (standards) of their use permitting their preservation *in the context of a given society*. For example, in the case of human beings, we will speak of their possibility to have a fulfilled or good life,[11] without danger and stress, coupled with their participation in the decisions of the firm. By "means to have a fulfilled or good life" or "good conservation in the context of a given society", we do not consider revenues of simple subsistence or of existence, or minimal revenues or even decent revenues, as it is the case in the frame of the capitalist philosophy of the "maintenance" of the cost of the work force.[12] We will show that these means correspond to payments that are *not considered as incomes* but as sums permitting the conservation of the people: the "true incomes" of these peoples will *begin only after assurance of their strict conservation* (see further in this chapter). This revolution will be realized in the frame of a drastic diminution of the differences of level of pays in all firms: we suggest to take account, in a first approach, of the proposal made by Giraud and Renouard (2017) of an initial maximum range of 12, progressively reduced to a range of 5 or 6. In the case of difficulties of the firms in providing for people to continue to have a fulfilled life, the possibility will be guaranteed through a national social fund financed by contributions of all the firms of the nation; so the firms *themselves* will thus be made collectively responsible for their acts.[13]

In the case of the elements of natural capital, it will be the task of scientists, notably ecologists, to define thresholds beyond which there are risks of loss of resilience of these elements (or group of elements) if these thresholds are transgressed. By reason of the practical difficulty to define these thresholds, a pragmatic solution will be to define zones where there is a risk of transgressing the thresholds. These zones will be conceived so that they can give signals of danger well before the effects of the limits of resilience. This kind of practical philosophy inspires the Swiss school of eco-points, developed notably by Müller-Wenck (1972) and, more recently, in the field of accounting for biodiversity, the writings of Ionescu (2016).[14] Without the definition of these norms (standards) it is impossible to assign a concrete objective to human and ecological management. Contrary to a frequent conception of CSR[15] management which does not set any limits (or zones) of use of the environmental and human capitals, the CARE/TDL method is guided by scientific limits determined on the basis of ontological studies. We consider that any management which is not coupled with these types of scientific objectives is voided to failure because it is "blind".[16] It is very often the case of the CSR which is generally based on tactical objectives or vague notions of progress without precise reference to scientific goals. Generally this kind of management leads to *half measures* because the causes of the problems are neither elucidated nor fully addressed. We can give two examples. Firstly, with regard to global warming, the firms concerned are at best only making *efforts* without respecting the Greenhouse gas reduction demanded by the IPCC (see further in this chapter). Secondly, in the case of the Covid-19 crisis, there is no question of being interested in the root causes of the occurrence of these types of viruses (fundamentally massive deforestation problems due to capitalist type of management), but of trying to cure ex post the health and social problems resulting from these practices. We do not deny that certain firms could have a serious policy of conservation of natural and human capitals in the frame of the CSR. We know that this concept has very different facets (Capron and Quairel, 2016, 16). But we think that the firms which really want to take CSR seriously should systematically apply the type of conservation of the capitals proposed by the CARE/TDL method, as it means a system based on the recognition of scientific targets. They will thus distinguish themselves from other firms which want only the pretence that they do something when they do nothing serious. The importance of human and ecological scientific targets had been already stressed in the 1950s by different authors such as Ciriacy-Wantrup (1952) with his concept of "the safe minimum standard" (SMS) and, before him, by Kapp. This author, also of German origin, wrote, as early as 1950, a remarkable book on the "social costs of private enterprise" which has anticipated the famous work of Bowen (1953), to whom is attributed the fathering of the concept of CSR.

His avant-garde conception of social costs is all the more interesting because, in contrast to Bowen, he proposes some innovations in matters of management and of economy of the firm that are already within the philosophy of the CARE/TDL method, notably the systematic use of scientific targets in matter of ecology[17](see Richard's preface to the new edition of his book in French in 2015 and the writings of Berger, notably his 2017 book). Kapp's ideas have later been followed and developed by Hueting (1980) and Ekins and Simon (1998): these ecological economists have proposed the use of limits as central elements of their macro-economic models of strong sustainability. So an economic literature already exists, unfortunately not frequently quoted and used, since the 1950s-70s, that goes well beyond the traditional theses and practices of CSR. More recently Gadrey and Jany-Catrice (2012), Méda (2013) and Gadrey and Lalucq (2015) have stressed in France the necessity to base the reform of the economy on physical, human and biological non-monetary indicators. And now the "Scientific Based Targets Initiative" has developed these ideas in the US. The CARE/TDL method is completely in line with these types of requirements which characterize true ecological economics. Gadrey and Lalucq (2015, 83) seem to believe that there is a conflict between the monetary approach of CARE and the "non-monetary methods founded on social and ecological norms" but this is not the case, as we will show. Indeed, the CARE method *goes further* than the non-monetary approaches. Its innovatory aspect, by comparison of all other writings, is two-fold. Firstly, it is to link in a systematic way the physical norms (or standards) with monetary concepts and indicators of capital and profit of business accounting. This monetary accounting perspective permits, at both the micro-economic and macro-economic levels, to have a true alternative to today's capitalist accounting (see further in this chapter).[18]Moreover, and secondly, in the frame of this micro-macro approach, the limits or zones of limits will be chiefly defined by the firms themselves under the control of independent auditors. This will allow a more specific and adapted range of indicators than those that could be defined from state authorities. Of course, in certain cases of phenomena of worldwide dimension the definition of targets will occur at the global level. This applies to the case of green-house gases (see further in this chapter). More generally, a cooperation of local, regional, national, and international organs or institutions will be necessary to achieve the task of defining ecological and social norms and standards of quality.

1–5 Fifth axiom: the necessity of a new kind of double entry accounting

We have seen that any correct management of a firm imposes a dualistic model with one side reserved for the conservation of the capitals and the other one for their use. It goes in the same way with the CARE/TDL model. But, in this model, the types of capitals have been multiplied by three (at least). Thus, we remain in the frame of a double entry accounting but with an extension of its application. We can observe, in this respect, that this kind of technique is a neutral one: it can be applied as well in the frame of capitalism as in that of a new ecological and human society. We thus dispute radically Habermas' thesis (1968) and more generally the modern German philosophy's thesis of "technique as an ideology". One must not confound a technique and its use. Classically, in our new balance sheet, the right side will be devoted to the registration of the amount of the capitals to be conserved and the results (past results accumulated and result of the last period of activity) and the left side to corresponding assets, the latter being defined as tangible or intangible things to be used for certain wants or desires.

1–6   Sixth axiom: the imposition of the new model by accounting laws

The appliance of the new models of balance sheets with three types of capital-debts should be made obligatory by accounting laws for all economic actors, beginning with the big international firms which are considered in this book as chiefly responsible for today's social and ecological situation. The capitalist system has succeeded in imposing a totally unreasonable economic system on humanity on the motive of its alleged "rationality". There is no reason to refuse to propose a truly reasonable obligatory economic system to replace it. We "only" propose the application of the same constraints that are already used today by capitalist firms. As it is generally the case today, simplified regimes will be provided for small firms. The generalization of these accounting obligations will permit progress rapidly and effectively towards the realization of ecological and human objectives demanded by more and more citizens in the world. Thus, we will end this terrible dualism that imposes strict laws for the conservation of financial capital and soft laws for the conservation of the two other types of capital. This accounting law solution could be coupled with the attribution of a personality to nature and its consideration as an "investor" of capital in companies (see further in this chapter).[19] This evolution of the law is already proposed in France by certain progressive lawyers such as Bardy (2017), author of an important dissertation on the concept of environmental debt in line with the CARE/TDL model.

1–7   Seventh axiom: the necessity of the systematic determination of sustainability gaps

Each economic entity, in order to establish its ecologic balance sheet (in a larger sense), will be obliged to make a comparison between the actual situation of its human and ecological capital and the local, regional, national and international standards of which it is answerable to. This comparison will permit to determine the gaps between their practices (notably in case of pollution, consumption and pay), and the human and ecological standards that they are supposed to respect. We will thus have two main types of monetary or non-monetary gaps: gaps relative to human sustainability and gaps for ecological sustainability. Let us underline, to finish with this proposal, that this type of action is a common thing in big businesses concerning financial capital when they keep budgets (forecasted accounts) to be compared with actual accounts. This leads us to the following point.

1–8 Eighth axiom: obligation to provide for budgets of preservation of all the capitals

In the case of human capital the firms will provide monthly budgets for the preservation of the people working inside the firm. In the case of the appearance of natural sustainability gaps (or better in the case of risk of such a circumstance) the concerned firms will have to first determine the least costly measures to be taken in order to remedy this situation and allow the concerned capitals to return to a state of resilience in the best way compatible with this resilience. Obviously, the best solution would be to avoid this situation and to have a "perfect" type of natural management which implies no sustainability gap.[20] In the case of sustainability gaps the firms will be obliged to measure and forecast, for each capital, taken separately, the budget of costs necessary for reaching a situation of sustainability (resilience). These budgets will be named "budgets of costs for sustainability (BCS)". Thus, generally, if the firm is not a perfect one in ecological matters, three main types of budgets will appear in the CARE/TDL model as soon as the formation of any firm: budgets for the financial, natural and human capitals. We want to stress that this concept of budget based on the respect of constraints for the sake of systematic conservation, notably of humans, has far-reaching consequences. It may involve very diverse and complex questions. We may give an example with the recent coronavirus crisis. It has been noted that with the capitalist form of internalization of economies, the production of some strategic resources such as medicinal products has been delocalized in low cost countries like China and India by the western firms for the sake of profitability. Such a situation has provoked very serious problems, notably a lack of basic instruments of protection against the extension of the virus in western countries. It is clear that in the frame of the CARE/TDL philosophy of systematic conservation of people, such choices concerning vital products cannot be accepted: there must be limits to the overall law of value even in the case of the CARE/TDL approach which foster the calculation of true costs. When, notably, the health of people is at stake, the question of minimal costs must be put aside and will be dominated by the question of security: this is in line with the principle of conservation fostered by CARE. Let us again underline that this philosophy is also a common one in financial accounting: we know that financial capital is systematically conserved, as a matter of principle.[21] As the reader can see, what we suggest in matters of human and natural capital is only an extension of old and traditional capitalist practices. This last point leads us to the following principle.

1–9 Ninth axiom: registration of the budgets of conservation costs as capitals in the balance sheet

The budgets of costs provided for the conservation of the different persons for a certain forecasted period will constitute the global human capital. This means the debt of the firm towards its personnel will be registered in the liabilities side of the balance sheet as human capital accounting. Similarly, the sum of budgets eventually provided for the conservation of natural capital will constitute what we call the "global natural capital" of the firm. This valuation of the capitals on the basis of conservation costs has nothing to do with the determination of their price on a market as is generally the case in economics. As said by Viveret, "true wealth has no price" (in Merlant et al., 2003, 57). As added by Richard (2013, 81), "nature has no price but its maintenance has a cost". More generally, Rambaud has demonstrated in his doctoral dissertation (2015) that *the value of existence of a thing is its cost of conservation.* Our philosophy of accounting has nothing to do with all those who want to give a price to "intangible" assets such as employees or *even to ethics* in the frame of the so-called search for the "value of values" (De Lastic, 2014): this is the culmination of the ideology of the financial model 2[22]! After all these registrations on the basis of conservation (preservation) costs, the new liabilities' side of the CARE/TDL model, contrary to its capitalist counterpart, will no longer consist in only one capital-debt (financial capital), but in three main types of capitals. We will see the appearance of three distinct lines (or zones or slides) of capitals relative to the natural, human and financial types of capital. Let us notice that the expression of "tri-capitalism" that can be attributed to the CARE/TDL model (Richard, 2012a) does not mean that there are only three capitals. As a matter of fact, each main type of capital, especially natural capital, can be composed of a multitude of capital elements. With this new kind of accounting there will be an "explosion" of the number of capitals. There is also, principally, no connection between these capitals. We have seen, indeed, that we rely on the hypothesis of strong sustainability. Consequently, these three zones will be "impermeable", without possible compensation between them. It will be the same for the case of its respective components, except, as mentioned before, for financial capital for which compensation is generally acknowledged. With this registration we can consider that there are now three types of capital contributions (or stakes) to the formation of a firm (company) at the micro or the macro level: the capital contributions made by nature, humans as persons and the providers of financial investments. This is a (considerable) extension of the traditional conception of the concept of stakes (contributions), traditionally reduced to financial stakes in the capitalist company law. We now consider that there are systematically *three kinds of associates who bring their capital contributions* to form a company. This new type of company is based on a new institutional device previously established in the context of a new constitutional process (see further in this chapter). It seems to us that this conception, in spite of some differences, presents many similarities with the famous theory of the gift as initiated by the French sociologist Marcel Mauss. In his essay, "The Gift" (1925) Mauss, on the basis of Malinowski (1922), shows that some Melanesian societies who practice the "kula" have non-merchant exchanges of gift and counter-gift which permit to assure the cohesion and the conservation of their type of society. We deem that we have a similar situation in the case of the CARE/TDL model as applied to human capital. Indeed, in this model, the employees make the (temporary) gift of their person to the firm in promise of a "return", or counter-gift: the (strict) conservation of their person. The gift received is registered as an asset to be used on the assets' side of the balance sheet while the counter-gift, the obligation of return (the conservation), is registered as a debt of the firm toward the employee on the liabilities' side. Thus, the mechanism of double entry becomes at the service of a non-merchant economy in line with the wishes of the sociologists defenders of the economics of the gift. The "Maussian CARE/TDL" balance sheet could appear in the following way as applied to human capital [23]:

Of course, here, at the difference of cases studied by Mauss and Malinowki, the gift concerns the people themselves and not some objects that are exchanged in the course of their activities. But the ethics are the same with a focus on the non-instrumental character of the relationships. More broadly, the general goal is similar: to found a type of society where the will to cooperate dominates in the frame of a co-management for a common goal[24]. Consequently our conception is a larger one than the Maussian conception: it does not only focus on individual exchanges made by persons

Table 1.1 Assets Liabilities

Gifts received to use a person	Gifts to give back: human capital to conserve

but also on the creation of an accounting constitution which is agreed by the people themselves and which governs all their acts, including their mode of participation to society (see further in this chapter). Another difference with the Maussian conception is that there is a strict equality of the gift and the counter-gift in the CARE/TDL method, which is not always the case in the practice of the Kula or other types of "primitive" exchanges.[25] As demonstrated by Chanial (2008), in reference to articles of Gouldner, the cases of disproportion between donators and receivers are often problematic. Caillé (2014, 45) also observes: "the danger . . . is that the gift crushes the receivers[26]". Florence Weber in her introduction to the work of Mauss (2007, 7–58) insists on the political stakes which are behind the positions of the "father" of the economics of the gift. She shows that Mauss wanted to find a solution in order to move away from the traditional system of patronage or charity which characterizes the capitalist world and create a system of social security which will give to everybody the means to live in a decent way (10–11). We believe that the CARE/TDL method can play this role. Besides the sociological sphere, the CARE/TDL method can also be related to the old religious thoughts, notably those of the Catholic creed. We have, notably, a special interest for a recent remarkable text of the Pope François: his encyclical letter "Laudato Si, the Care of the common house" (2015). The Pope underlines that some passages of Genesis invite to "cultivate and keep the garden of the world"(cf. Gn 2,15). The Pope infers from this phrase that while the verb "cultivate" refers to plough, clear the soil, or work, the verb "keep" means protect, safeguard, preserve, care, watch, which implies that "each community may draw out the goodness of the soil that is necessary for it to survive, but it also has the obligation to keep and guarantee the continuity of its fertility for the future generations" (53–54).[27] This dualistic view corresponds to the double entry concept of traditional accounting: use some assets while conserving the capital. This type of thought is all the more in line with the CARE/TDL model given that the Pope insists on the respect of *limits* imposed by the renewal of the soil. Indeed, the Pope often uses the vocabulary of "points of rupture" and "limits" to be respected. This is notably the case when he is very critical to the financiers: "the belief in the infinite availability of the goods of the planet . . . leads to press it up to the limits and even beyond the limits" (83). In line with the Bishops of Portugal, the Pope concludes that "the environment lies in the logic of the reception. It is a loan that each generation receives and must transmit to the following generation" (122–123). The traditional accounting view applied in the CARE/TDL model is also based on these notions of loan and debt. To conclude on this point, we may ascertain that many different conceptions of society, religious ones or not, are conceived on the same basis as the CARE/TDL method. The latter provides the possibility *to integrate these philosophies in the frame of a monetary economy.* It will notably permit to reconstruct the concept of cost and to adapt it to a human and ecological society.

1–10 Tenth axiom: registration of a full cost of preservation (conservation)

In accordance with the system of double entry accounting, simultaneously and symmetrically to the registration of the amounts of the three capital-debts on the liabilities' side of the balance sheet, the same amounts will be registered on the asset's side as *costs of usage* of these capitals, as assets to be used. The progressive use of these assets will imply, in a classical way, the appearance of three main types of depreciation. The diminution of these assets, also, classically, will have as counterpart the registration of corresponding depreciation expenses, to represent the diminution of the respective capitals.[28] Thus, in the new P&L statement we will see the appearance of three (main) separated lines of depreciation expenses corresponding to the use of the three types of capital. This can explain the denomination of the CARE/TDL method: TDL means "triple depreciation line" (instead of only one[29] in the capitalist model). Thanks to the registration of these three types of expenses we will obtain a true full cost (human, ecological and financial) which will be thoroughly different from the truncated cost of today's capitalist world.[30] This new type of cost will be the basis of the formation of new types of prices, allowing for the conservation of humans and nature. It will be at the origin of a totally different type of market. A market without any more discarding to the detriment of nature and of people, a plague which characterizes, since its origin, the capitalist world. All the firms will be obliged to price their products at the minimum of their "full" cost as redefined by the CARE/TDL method. This will be a totally different situation from the one which is regulated by the WTO (World Trade Organization) on the basis of the capitalist truncated cost.[31] Normally, the firm which will price its products along this type of new, full cost will receive an amount of money that will permit it to reinvest in the three main different capitals that have been used, so that it can conserve them all; this will be the end of the privilege of financial capital. This will also be the end of the distribution to shareholders of fictitious gains: the end of this capitalist world mainly characterized by a huge distribution of fictitious profits. As already explained, the CARE/TDL method is based on ecological and human non-monetary indicators. But it also permits the rebuilding of all the monetary indicators of firms (costs, profits, added value, return on investment, etc.); it is the basis of a new type of market economy. Among the main beneficiaries of this drastic change will be the ecological farmers. They will no longer be obliged to implore subsidies to survive, or taxes against unequal competition, or even so called "payments for environmental services[32]" (see the next section for our criticism of this liberal-capitalist invention). They will be paid on the basis of their true costs and have a "good" life and the protection of their lands.[33] As said by Mauss (quoted by F. Weber, 2007, 10), it is necessary to get out of "the unconscious and injurious patronage of the rich chaplain".[34] The consecration of this true cost will notably permit to conceive a new concept of profit.

1–11   Eleventh axiom: a new type of profit, a profit for the commons

The new type of firms which will emerge thanks to the application of the CARE/TDL method will have the possibility to make profits, but, as we have demonstrated, new types of profits which are not gained to the detriment of natural and human capitals. Some of these new firms, if they are managed in an intelligent way, will have lower costs than their competitors: the CARE/TDL method forbids ecological and human discarding but it does not forbid a *sane competition*. In that case these efficient firms will have a profit: a justified, ecological and human profit in the frame of this new type of market economy. They will also have a return on equity, but a new one. It will no longer be the capitalist financial return calculated on the basis of the comparison of financial profit and financial equity (sum of financial capital and retained earnings). This new return will be calculated by comparing the new type of profit with the *global mass* of the three types of new capitals. Max Weber (1920a and 1920b) had not practically formulated the possibility of an alternative model to capitalism with a specific measure of the return on investment for social and ecological aims. He had wrongly believed that the calculation of capital (Kapitalrechnung) and the return on equity (Rentabilität) of capitalists were (unavoidably) features of any rational economy (Protestant ethic, German version page 11; French version page 11–13). As a matter of fact, these instruments of rationalization can be used in the frame of another society with new concepts of profit and capitals. As far as profit is concerned we have seen that the CARE/TDL profit is conceived in a totally different way as capitalist profit, on the basis of a different concept of cost. But this is not the only one aspect of its novelty. Indeed, as far as it results from the common activity of three types of capitals it will be considered as a *common profit* to the three capitals. Thus, the CARE/TDL method results in a common earning of these three capitals. This conception can be considered as a realization of the ideas formulated by Ostrom (1990). It seems to us that the CARE/TDL method will offer the possibility to give concrete expression to the wishes of Ostrom to see the multiplication of common firms. The existence of this common profit will not make the firm a community in the sense of Gierke (1868, 116–117) with a common consciousness (Gemeinbewusst-sein); there will also be conflicts of interest in the frame of the CARE/TDL model as they exist in the frame of the capitalist world, notably conflicts opposing those who think long term to others preferring short-term results. But it is probable that, with time, these conflicts will be of a lesser degree due to the existence of this common profit calculated under the constraint of the conservation of three capitals. This new accounting approach should be realized at the global level (see the next section), not in certain sectors of the economy only. This will permit the social and solidarity economy and the enterprise in common to dominate the economic arena. Today, unfortunately, they have a small chance to develop in a world where the capitalist firms constantly practice social and ecological discarding.

1–12 Twelfth axiom: towards an ecological co-management

The application of the preceding proposals will have profound conse-quences in the matter of governance of firms. Firstly, with CARE, each type of capital has its *own depreciation expenses:* each one is at the expense of its own capital. This is particularly the case of human capital. The deprecia-tion of human assets corresponds to an expense of human capital, not that of financial capital as is the case with capitalist accounting. Secondly, the appearance of three types of capitals instead of one (financial capital) in the liabilities' side leads to the consideration that there are *three kinds of inves-tors* in a firm that must be treated on an equal footing, notably in the matter of power. If capital is power, all types of capital must have power! Thus, in the CARE/TDL model, as will be explained in more detail later in this chapter, the representatives of the three capitals will have equal power in all key decisions, at all levels of the firm, notably in matters of decisions which concern the choice of managers and the distribution of (new) profit. This will be an *ecological co-management* of a completely new type, which goes much far beyond the famous German co-determination.[35] The investors in human capital will no longer be mere wage receivers. They will all become *partners* of the firm like the investors of financial capital. Capitalism has the gift of monopolizing all the flattering terms. The capitalists describe them-selves as active "investors", "associates", "givers of work" (Arbeitgeber in German), "employers", "risktakers" while the workers are not investors, not associates but only passive "takers of work" (Arbeitnehmer in German), or employees and do not take any risks. With the CARE/TDL system they also become investors, associates and risktakers. There is a kind of tran-scendence of capitalism through tri-capitalism: all investors become new "capitalists" in the sense of very important persons or things that are to be systematically preserved and have an equal right of participation in the firm. This will be the real recognition of employees as human beings in firms as wished by Honneth (1992/2005) and Fraser (2005). This will bring the possibility of a drastic transformation of their work in the firm with true creative activity as wished by Castoriadis (1975). Contrary to the famous thesis of Arendt (1958) it is possible, in spite of the presence of machines, to transform the task of workers from repetitive and senseless activities into something else if they have the right to be heard on the organization of their work and, more largely, to decide on the goals of the firm. We underline that, in contrast with the traditional Marxist views in question, the suppliers of financial capital conserve the right of participation into the affairs of the firm, albeit a very substantially reduced right in comparison with the capitalist system. For us the total eviction of the financial investors from power is a double theoretical and practical error. It is firstly a theoretical mistake which is due to Marx himself making a drastic distinction between dead and living labour: dead labour, like a vampire, sucks the life of living labour, the latter being the only source of the creation of wealth. But as demonstrated by the libertarian communist Cornelissen in his original theory of value (1913, 152–153), it is necessary to take account of the work of past generations which permits the creation of value today: both living and dead labour participate in the creation of new value.[36] Let us underline that today's promoters of workers' cooperatives have ratified the views of Cornelissen rather than those of Marx. Indeed they have accepted that in these cooperatives the workers could invest, and even, in many countries, must invest their past "accumulations" of money to build these types of firms. We approve this philosophy of popular investments. Thus, if a former worker of a firm conceived along the CARE/TDL model has made economies and accepts to invest them in his former firm why should he been deprived of any participation in the decisions of this firm, beginning with the control of the reality of conservation of his financial capital? It is a practical error because it prevents the possibility of a larger and popular self-financing of firms from the part of workers and employees, which should be encouraged in the frame of a new economy where the big capitalists have lost their former monopoly of power.[37]We will show that the danger of monopoly power from the part of these popular investors is much reduced if not totally reduced in the frame of our new model of firm (see the next section). We conclude on this point that the CARE conception of new financial capital is a kind of extension of the practice of today's worker cooperatives at the national and world level. Indeed, in these cooperatives there is generally an investment of financial capital of the workers which is made on the basis of their past economies, its means are dead labour. CARE/TDL must be understood as a system of governance that extends at the global level the old concept of workers' cooperatives, however with an ecological "touch" that takes account of the necessity of the strict preservation and representation of natural capital. This will permit the avoidance of the recourse to debt financing within the frame of bank institutions that are generally in the hands of bureaucrats, even if representatives of workers of these banks take share in the power. We also underline that we believe that it is necessary to introduce specific representatives of natural capital. History has shown that trade unions are not obligatory defenders of this type of capital. Coutrot (2010, 204) gives the example of the German Federation of Trade Unions of the chemical industry which "has made a common front with industrials against ecologists to prevent the implementation of the REACH European Directive". Owing to this kind of fact it seems to us better to have three separate sets of representatives for the three types of capitals, a case which does not prevent some "ecological" employees or residents to participate in the cause of the protection of natural capital (see further in this chapter). Thus, for us, there are three categories of investors who are associated in a new type of company with *specific* representatives. This assertion permits us to develop the concept of a *"CARE/TDL integral capital-holder theory*: the ITCH" (in French, "Théorie Intégrale des Investisseurs de Capitaux, TIIC"). This new theory of corporate governance will replace the dominating American "Stake-Holder Theory"(Richard, 2012, 2016). We will demonstrate later that this "Capital-Holder Theory" is much more precise and adapted to today's ecological and human crisis than the inexact and limited Stake-Holder Theory. First and foremost, it relies on a system of accounting which permits the clear identification of investors (or capital holders) of the firm and to measure the results of their common activity. This new system of accounting may be described synthetically by Figure 1.2.

As the reader may see in this synthetic diagram the two non-financial capitals, here grouped under the denomination of "extra financial capital", are now present on the liabilities' side of the balance sheet (on the right of the box symbolizing the firm). The interaction of the financial and the extra-financial capitals gives way to mixed assets (green colour in the box), which will be sold and thus will permit the acquisition of new resources, allowing for the maintenance of all capitals and eventually some common profit.

With this last diagram we have finished the presentation of the bases of our CARE/TDL model. It intends to be a marked innovation at the service of ecological and human causes which can permit the birth of a new "homo economicus". As Mauss (1925, 238) stated, the "homo economicus is not behind us, he is before us". We will have a new accounting system under the constraint of the preservation (conservation) of three types of capitals which normally could satisfy all defenders of a new ecological and democratic society, as well as religious believers and atheists.[38]We will now comment on some initiatives

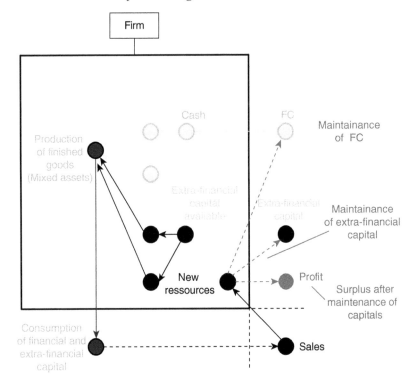

Figure 1.2 The Care/TDL Method: Synthesis

Source: Rambaud

which aim to guarantee the survival of the capitalist system under the guise of progressivism. If applied they will result in a loss of precious time at a moment when mankind has a need for drastic decisions to solve urgent problems.

Notes

1 Initially this model has been conceived by Jacques Richard in 2008 and published in a book in 2012 (Comptabilité et Développement Durable Ed Economica Paris) then largely improved with the help of Alexandre Rambaud (see the bibliography). It can be now considered as a common work.

2 "The starting point has to be the elaboration of goals notably fundamental requirements of human life".

3 Unfortunately today the most famous and well known representation is proposed by main stream economists, which is totally influenced by the capitalist ideology. It consists in three *sequential* circles representing the financial capital, the human capital and the natural capital. It means, practically, that the conservation of human capital and natural capital depend on the satisfaction of the

"appetites" of the financial capital, a hypothesis that we totally reject (see Richard and Plot, 2014, 10–14).

4 Each broad category of capital may comprise many different parts as it is already the case today for the financial capital.

5 This position has been somewhat anticipated by early medieval scholars like Jean Duns Scott (1266–1308). This Franciscan monk wanted to take systematical account of the conservation of the work force for the determination of the prices of products. He clashed with Thomas d'Aquin (1225–1274), who deemed (well before Adam Smith) that the prices should be fundamentally determined by the market movements. He probably inspired Coux (1832), one of the rare economists of his time who wanted to submit economics to ethics. Schumpeter considered this scholastic debate as the origin of economic science (See Sivéry, 2004).

6 In Greek "axios" means what is worth to be considered.

7 The idea of limits of use is very old; it can be found in Plato. But Plato has never included this kind of idea into economic laws. He has only expressed very general principles (Republic, 1993, 122 and 366).

8 We are aware of the famous American debate between "conservationists" and "preservationists". If we had to choose we will prefer the term preservation. But the main thing is to explain the sense of the words which will be used. Thus we ask our readers to pay attention first to *the use* we make of these words.

9 Resilience can be defined by the maximum of intensity that a system can bear without changing its behaviour, when it conserves the same structure, the same functions and the same responses.

10 We believe that this conception is in line with the views defended by Nussbaum (1990) and Nussbaum and Sen (1990).The difference is that we include the notion of capability into the frame of an accounting system which change radically the notions of profit and markets, and proposes an ecological and humane governance.

11 Renouard (2013, 43) defines the ethics as the search for a good life. Aristotle already spoke of "eu-daimonia" in his Nicomachean Ethics. We will show later that our concept of a good life is not tied with a question of happiness, but good conservation.

12 The reflections made by Corning (2011, chapter 5) on this subject will be notably precious ones. This author advices to take account of 13 basic indicators concerning thermoregulation, waste elimination, nutrition, water, mobility, sleep, respiration, physical safety, physical health, mental health, social relationships, reproduction and nurturance of offspring. In the same way specialists of the ILO (international Labour Organization) such as Anker and Alii (ILO, 2011) propose a list of 11 statistical indicators of decent work.

13 It seems to us that these considerations may be compatible with some of the views defended by Friot (2012).

14 Castoriadis (1975, 133) underlines that practitioners admit that they do not know everything to the difference of many philosophers. This is the case of accountants who are conscious of the limits of their art.

15 Corporate Social Responsibility.

16 In the same way that in financial accounting it is not possible to determine the depreciation of machines or planes without scientific studies of the level of use of these elements.

17 In the 1963 edition of his book Kapp, contrary to Pigou and Coase, refuses the recourse to cost benefit analysis and to the internalization of externalities to treat the environmental problems. He suggests, as Care does, applying the accounting

method of depreciation to the men and the animals like the whales! He prefers the prevention and the valuation of ecological assets in terms of maintaining costs on the basis of ecological norms (Richard, 2015, 19–26; Kapp, 1963, chapters 6,7, 8 and 15 on the problem of social value and social choices).

18 In any case, in a market society, a firm which will seriously take account of non-monetary limits will be obliged to calculate the cost of these measures and to integrate them in a new type of monetary accounting, a task which is not obvious if the different capitals are separately conserved and if their conservation is to be checked in a clear accounting way, as is the case for financial capital. The CARE/TDL method gives a theoretical and practical framework for such a change, which is not the case of the economists, even ecological ones.

19 On the contrary it does not seem to be pertinent to have recourse to the concept of common good: a good is an asset to be used, not a capital-debt to be conserved. There is a contradiction between the idea of conservation and the concept of good, even common good.

20 In the case of the perfect management of a firm which does not destroy the natural capital there will be no natural debt and, hence, no budget. This case will be rare today.

21 Concretely, the traditional accounting system provides for the possibility that, at the time of the formation of a firm, a budget of "capital" (to be conserved) will appear on the liabilities' side of the balance sheet with a counterpart on the assets' side under the denomination: "capital subscribed, not yet paid".

22 See Volume 1 (The true nature of capitalism).

23 In the case of natural capital, nature has no personality but nevertheless the firm borrows from its resources and has to return to it on behalf of its declaration to respect its conservation (see the list of axioms). If this accounting constitution is legally accepted this device is sufficient to apply the theory of the gift to natural capital. The gift and the counter-gift are rational internal engagements of the firms ratified by the collectivity of humans. There is thus no necessity to have recourse to the responsibility towards future generations as does Jonas (1979), and even to a personification of the mother nature as it is proposed by numerous lawyers.

24 Including a common profit (in the sense of the CARE method).

25 Sahlins (1972, 164–168) also speaks of unequal exchange in the frame of Maori customs. Some yield ("hau") has to be given above the capital ("mauri").

26 In a general way we know from the German word "gift" that it can be a poison!

27 We see here that the ethical claims of Jonas (1979) have been anticipated by these old religious texts!

28 Of course, here capitals are the capital-debts not the capitals as assets of economists!

29 Of course by only one we mean only *one type* concerning the financial capital in his globality, with a lot of components relative to diverse objects: machines, tools, buildings, etc.

30 We remind that Kapp (1950) characterizes capitalism as an economic system that does not pay its costs.

31 Under the rules of the WTO, no firm must price a product under its (truncated) capitalist cost. Trespassing of this rule is severely condemned. Thus, no discarding is possible as far as the financial capital is concerned !

32 Etrillard (2015).

33 More generally, the emergence of real costs and their appliance at the global level will permit to make an end to the social and environmental dumpings. The consequence will be a drastic reallocation of activities.

34 This evolution towards a true ecological and human cost is recommended by the commission of the agriculture of the French state-institution CESE (Conseil Economique Social et Environnemental).

35 Askenazy (2016, 186–187) shows that German co-determination did not allow for the prevention of the rise of financial capitalism and the resurgence of poverty. The power granted to the shareholders remained too big.

36 We thank Jourdain (2019) to have reminded us of this author.

37 The new ecological and human firms should have a big interest in the financial participation of new types of shareholders respectuous of the conservation of the three types of capital.

38 We notably believe that there is no major contradiction of our views with those of the defenders of the idea of "Degrowth" such as notably Latouche (2010). Latouche, like us, constantly speaks of the respect of limits and finitude and of abandonment of the capitalist imaginary (133 and 189). If there is a difference it is that CARE proposes an alternative to the capitalist system while Degrowth is more dedicated to indicate the possible means of actions (such as recycling) at the local level. Latouche indeed considers that "it is impossible to frontally overthrow capitalism" (2010, 276). We contest this assertion.

2 Presentation of some misleading solutions conceived by capitalists and their allies

The social and environmental crises which mark the beginning of the 21st century oblige capitalists to react to the numerous critics of all their victims. Sometimes, some of them are even victims of their own actions such as the billionaire Trevor Neilson whose town has been burnt in big fires. However, as shown in a vivid way by Gaël Giraud,[1] most of them are able to find solutions to their personal problems. The main thing for them is to show that they do something to persuade people that capitalism is the solution for the misfits of capitalism. It is imperative for them to demonstrate that they make endeavours to cope with the crises. For example the billionaire mentioned before has launched a Climate Emergency Fund for encouraging associations that have disruptive actions in favour of the climate. Thus the arsonist transforms himself into a firefighter! As Edouard Morena underlines, this type of action does not question the system itself and the power behind it (Le Monde, 17/8/2019, 9). This remark is also valid for the case of apparently more serious collective actions. We have already spoken of the famous CSR and of its limits. We will thus not speak any longer of so called "responsible finance", or socially responsible investment (SRI). It relies on the idea that some enlightened shareholders will choose to invest in companies which make endeavours for the human and ecological cause. The experience has shown that this kind of solution has, notably, not permitted to reduce the emission of green-house gasses[2]. If these shareholders were really responsible they should promote solutions such as the CARE/TDL method, which would permit them to avoid a choice of "best in class" investors; all firms would become obliged to be responsible. However this traditional idea of a mutation of the mind of financial capitalists on their own initiative is constantly put back on the agenda by the socialists and the liberals who bear the responsibility for the current environmental and social crises, in particular because of their unreserved support to the concoction of the IFRS standards that lead the economic world. Thus Attali (2020), the former economic adviser of Mitterand, speaks out recently for a new

DOI: 10.4324/9781003194149-4

"economy of life" without ever questioning the power of shareholders in large firms. We will now discuss proposals that belong to the category of the accounting or economic type. They apparently aim to achieve similar objectives to the CARE/TDL model and, thus, merit a comparison with it. Among them we will have a special interest for those which are very fashionable today such as the "theory of the internalization of externalities", the carbon taxes, the "carbon pricing mechanism", "Integrated Reporting" and the taxation of rich people.

2–1 The taxation of rich people

One of the most recent repeats of this old idea is contained in the book of Saez and Zucman (2019) about "The triumph of injustice". They notably propose a doubling of the taxation on the fortunes of very rich people. This classical proposal is problematic if it is taken alone as a solution for eliminating capitalists, or at least reducing their influence on economics. History has shown that this type of measure has not permitted a change in strategy of capitalist firms. The main problem of capitalism is not that it makes some people rich, but that it destroys the planet and also people, because of the exclusive *power* of capitalists in the firms. The taxation of rich people *will not change this situation.* Even from the point of view of the promoters of this kind of measure, its rationality is very curious: why first give the possibility to these people to earn a lot of money to the detriment of the other investors and afterward take some measures to try to remedy the situation somewhat? As Pech (2017, 227) underlines, "the march towards equity cannot consist in correcting the disparities after the fact". In reality, with this approach, the goal is not to find a solution to the real problem: the capitalist type of management will continue, even if it appears to be less scandalous. Without speaking of the unsupportable charitable character of this type of measure (the Rich, through the mediation of the State, concede a part of their wealth to the Poor), we consider that it is a means which permits the perpetuation of the capitalist model and offers no serious solution to today's crisis; it tends, on the contrary, to reinforce capitalism by giving to the capitalists the appearance to have been obliged to concede something secondary for preserving the essential: their power in the firms.

2–2 The theory of the internalization of externalities

The concept and the vocabulary of "externalities" have been promoted (coined) by the neoclassical economist Pigou (1932). They have gained a large audience, with a large publicity made by mainstream economists. They tend today to become neutral synonyms of all environmental and social problems and of their efficient treatment. However, this theory of externalities is clearly an element of the neoclassical economic theory which is at the basis of the capitalist economy (Harribey, 1998, chapter 4; Richard, 2012). Méda (1999, 52) justly underlines that it is connected to a utilitarian conception according to which pollution is not an evil which menaces all of us, but an individual problem to be treated (negotiated) by a polluter and a polluted. As shown by Richard (2012) and Rambaud (2015), it is a kind of cost-benefit analysis which consists in the comparison of the costs of measures taken for these kinds of problems with the value of the damages which will be avoided by these actions (the avoided damages being assimilated to benefits).These damages are generally perceived as economic damages resulting from "environmental problems". This is an anthropocentric capitalist view of the environment which has nothing to do with the question of the risks of destruction of the ecosphere as itself and the solutions to avoid these risks. Moreover, as these damages (loss of resources due to pollutions, etc.) are, most of the time, differed or located over many years, this type of economic analysis obligatorily uses the so called "methods of discounting" in order to make a comparison of the immediate costs (the cost of the protection measures taken today) to the future benefits (the future damages avoided). Discounting, one of the basic tools of capitalist economists since the time of Pacioli (see our Volume 1), relies on the integration of a norm of capitalist profitability in the reasoning: it means the integration of a minimal rate of return (or "cost" of financial capital). The fundamental idea is that a future amount of money is worth less than the same amount available today because the latter amount, if invested in capitalist financial markets, may return benefits in accordance with the interest rate on these markets. If this type of reasoning is applied to human and environmental problems the resolution of these problems depends of the dimension of the rate of return demanded by capitalists! Thus mainstream economists, who apparently want to deal with human and environmental problems, have succeeded in imposing a sufficient rate of capitalist profit, by way of a totally subjective and egoist constraint, as a condition of any social or ecological measure. With this kind of economic invention these "rational" economists are able to demonstrate in a "scientific way" that we must destroy plants and animals because the investment of the money made from their destruction provides interest (Clark, 1971; Conrad, 2010). Such is the very lesson of this terrible theory of externalities for whom many people of good faith have a great respect if not admiration. As a matter of fact, this theory is totally inappropriate for the treatment of today's problem, notably environmental problems, as is already shown by a rich critical literature (see notably Pearce, 1976; Richard, 2012; Rambaud, 2015). Our argumentation is also that of Pope François who in his encyclical "Laudato si" (2015) affirms that if human beings and environmental entities have non-instrumental values they must be conserved without conditions and, consequently, without recourse to sordid questions relevant of financial rates of profits (see on this peculiar topic of the Pope's position Christophe and Richard, 2018). Consequently, one must, with the Pope, reject this dreadful theory of the externalization of externalities. A true solution of ecological problems must rely on the registration of costs of conservation (preservation) of the ecosphere. As Rambaud has demonstrated in his doctoral dissertation (2015) the true value of existence of a thing consists in its cost of conservation.

2–3 The mechanism of carbon taxes

We have seen that a new concept of full cost based on ecological constraints is at the basis of the CARE/TDL model. This type of cost has nothing to do with a price formed on a market. It is an accounting construction made inside the firm and by the firm, operated in taking account of the constraint of the systematic conservation of three types of capitals, notably natural capital. As in every classical accounting this cost will form the basis of the fixation of prices and thus impose to the markets a regulation of its formation. This new accounting constraint is to be applied by every firm. In this kind of procedure the first and the main constraint to respect nature weights on the firms, the producers and not the final consumers. The goal is to make a rapid change of the production model with innovations adapted to the nature of ecological problems. This is a task which the consumers are unable to conceive alone[3], even more than the great mass of engineers are hired by the big firms. It is time, as already proposed by Kapp (1950), to put the technological progress *under the constraint* of a new economic system.[4] The CARE/TDL model makes the producers totally responsible for their acts, as they seem to claim if we hear their constant declarations in the frame of their great desire of CSR. This solution is at odds with that one proposed by the defenders of environmental taxes. These taxes are most often a pure product of the neo-classical thought, notably, again, of the English economist Pigou (1932). From a theoretical point of view they are based on the theory of internalization of externalities: integration of the discounted cost of pollutions (damages) in the demand curves. Thus, generally, as is the case, for example, of taxes concerning cars, they will hit consumers with the objective of avoiding creating difficulties for producers. They are not adapted to the nature of the problem for three main reasons. Firstly, these are the policies of production and marketing which are essentially at the root of today's problems. Most of the time consumers, especially the large mass of popular consumers, are unable to choose the products they consume due to low revenues. They will systematically take what is offered at the lowest price. In this context, these are the policies of production of the firms which are chiefly at the root of the problems, not the choice of the consumers. Secondly, these tax instruments are not flexible enough to take account of the diversity of the situations. Theoretically the level of the amount of tax should be personalized through the function of a multiplicity of criteria: type and age of the car, conditions of its use (notably the speed), length of the use, possibility or not of access to public modes of transportation, level of wealth, etc. This would imply a multiplicity of rates of taxes and excises: practically an impossible thing. This is why, generally, the choice is simple: to tax the consumption of fuel consumed. Thirdly, even if the preceding conditions were met this would not change the problem: that of a necessity of a drastic change of technologies from the part of the producers of cars. Indeed, the level of taxation on "car consumption" has no direct relation to a change of the type of cars offered on the market and the reduction of greenhouse gases: we can imagine that in rich countries an enormous mass of rich consumers will continue to prefer the use of polluting cars despite heavy taxes on the cars or their use. The only thing that could solve the problem would be to oblige the producers to produce ecological cars or, even better, to diversify their investments and collaborate with other industrials such as railway-producers. At this stage of the reasoning the reader could object that the use of these types of taxes could be reported on producers instead of consumers. This would be better but again not satisfactory because of the uncertain relation between the level of this taxation and the type of production offered by the producers of cars. This leads us to the last and third argument. Let us compare the solutions taken in the capitalist system for the conservation of natural and financial capital. As far as the latter is concerned we have seen that the firm is obliged to conserve it in any case by the companies and accounting laws. This is a strict obligation of the firm: no question here to tax the products to change the behaviour of the consumers. This a serious and effective measure taken by the capitalists themselves with the support of their allies. This has nothing to do with the procrastination of environmental taxes which only serve to avoid a direct and strict treatment of the problem.

2–4 Carbon pricing

Pottier (2016) has shown "how economists warm the planet" and are unable to propose a solution to cope with the ecological crisis. We will describe how accountants, with the help of the CARE/TDL model, may rapidly cool the planet. The fact is that we observe the same deviance from serious solutions in matters of global solutions in relation to green-house gasses (GHG). The neoclassic environmentalist economists have imagined a market for carbon with a price resulting from the exchanges of quotas, from rights to emit GHG in certain limits. The firms which can reduce their emissions below the limits can sell their rights on this market to those who are unable to. These economists cannot but put markets prices overall, even in matters of ecology. This "merchandising of carbon" has nothing to do with an efficient respect of the protection of the atmosphere, for four main reasons. Firstly, the limits which are to be observed aren't scientific limits such as those recommended by the IGEC: they are only limits corresponding to strategic or tactical goals, at best to improve somewhat or, rather, as documented by the IGEC, to maintain today's situation. Secondly, firms can escape their obligations by buying quotas on the market. The alleged advantage is invoked, as usual, in the name of a cost-benefit analysis: the firms that have lower costs of reduction of the gases will do the job for those whose costs are higher. But this kind of reasoning is both lacunar and static. It gives a bad signal to the "bad" firms to continue their business as usual and stirs them to delay the necessary changes that they should have made; it, thus, brakes their innovations, as is demonstrated by the failure described by Pottier. Thirdly the basic price is generally calculated by discounting the value of future economic damages due to global warming, which leads again to mix economic problems (the use of a rate of return for discounting and the damages *for the economy*) with ecological matters. Fourthly this solution is at odds with the classical view of capitalist accounting concerning financial capital. For this type of capital, invested, for example, in machines, there is no possibility for a "bad" firm to buy on a market the lower depreciation costs of another "efficient" firm in order to avoid the registration of its own higher costs. What does the CARE/TDL model propose in this matter?[5] That each firm will calculate its own "costs (not prices) of carbon" on the basis of the cost of the measures necessary to reduce its GHG emissions under the limits fixed by the IGEC and register these costs in its accounting according to the 12 principles presented earlier. The rise of its costs will reduce the profits distributed and permit the financing of the measures demanded by the IGEC. Thus, with this serious and efficient method, there will be as many "carbon costs" as there are firms. Traditional accountants have found efficient methods not based on market prices to permit the conservation of financial capital. It is time that their tools were put at the service of human and natural capitals. All the progressive forces should let aside the misleading solutions proposed by the mainstream neo classical economists, notably environmental taxes and carbon pricing.

2–5 Payments for environmental or ecological services

This idea has emerged under the influence of environmental economists who have tried to give a value (price) to nature.[6] In theory, since the services rendered by nature have a value (see further in this chapter) it seems normal that people who endeavour to conserve nature should be paid for this (OCDE, 2011; Karsenty et al., 2009). But the concrete initiatives in this field are tied with pragmatic situations. The most typical ones are the cases of cities which are confronted with polluted waters because of the pollution of the agricultural lands around these cities. They have two main possible solutions (in the absence of regulation). Either to pay for the construction of special cleaning stations or to pay the farmers who are responsible for pollution to change their practices; the latter case is payments for ecological services or, more exactly, for environmental services.[7] This reasoning relies, most of the time, on a cost-benefit analysis: the cities will opt for the payments to the farmers if they are less costly than the construction of cleaning devices. Generally, the cities will try to pay only the supplementary costs of the farmers for avoiding pollution, but if the farmers are good negotiators, they may obtain more. This example concerns public institutions, but it can also be found in the private sector. A famous case is that of the firm Vittel which has paid farmers around its sources of mineral water for measures permitting the conservation of these sources (Hellec, 2015). This kind of solution raises several problems.[8] Firstly, it results in contractual agreements and thus cannot have such a large application as in the case of mandatory application. Secondly, in this narrow context, it only concerns the cases when the cities or firms have an interest to engage in this solution in the frame of the cost-benefit analysis. Thirdly, it may encourage people who intend to engage freely in possible actions for preserving the environment to stop their endeavours in order to be paid for their "services". Fifthly, it will dishearten those who have already made the efforts to realize the ecological revolution. Sixthly, it is mainly proposed in the frame of economic problems, not pure ecological problems. In fact, the whole philosophy of this kind of solution is of ill nature and unfair. It is of ill nature because it considers it the norm to destroy natural capital (to have "externalities") and that we must "pay" people to stop this destruction. We can compare this solution with one of parents who give banknotes to their children for good behaviour at home or in class[9]: it is in line with a society where almost everything is commodified (except for financial capital in accounting). It is unfair because it is at odds with the solution which prevails in the matter of protection of financial capital. Indeed, in that case, there is no payment for the conservation of this type of capital. The reasoning of *traditional* capitalists is totally different. As previously demonstrated they consider that they themselves have the obligation to conserve their financial capital and they calculate their selling price on the basis of a cost of production, which integrates the preservation of their capital. They do not implore the government to pay for "services" that they give in conserving their capital: they do what is necessary to conserve it and obey to the laws of capitalist accounting. Thus, there is an obligatory and

systematic conservation without help and not, as is the case with the payments for environmental services, a bargaining of payments for "services"
rendered to natural capital. The CARE/TDL method permits the application
of capitalist conservation of financial capital to the other types of capitals:
this is the only one fair and effective solution, which can be coupled with
the action of specific taxes (see the following section). This is this solution,
implying the redefinition of the cost of products to include the conservation
of natural capital, which is recommended by the French Economic, Social
and Environmental Council[10]: to oblige firms which buy products of the
farmers to pay the true costs of these products. This will be the end of the
charity system of the payments for environmental services.

2–6   Integrated Reporting (IR) of the IIRC
(International Integrated Reporting Council)

This new type of reporting has recently gained the favour of many people
because it permits them to imagine that capitalist firms will treat their different capitals equally. Indeed the conceptual framework of the IIRC considers six types of capital (financial, manufactured, natural, human, social and
intellectual).[11] At first sight it seems a very interesting tool all the more as
it does not content itself to protect three types of capitals, as it is the case
of the CARE/TDL method, but six: what an ambition! But the bright form
hides a poor content which, after careful inspection, appears to be completely contradictory with the ambitious declaration to treat the six capitals
on an equal footing. We justify this criticism with five points (see for more
details Rambaud and Richard, 2015a). Firstly, IR does not deserve its name:
its reporting is not integrated to an ecological and human *accounting system*
as it is the case of the CARE/TDL reporting. Secondly, as a consequence
of the preceding remark, IR cohabits with the IFRS. The IIRC has never
denounced or even criticized these capitalist financial standards that are
particularly dangerous and obsolete (see Volume 1).Thirdly, it appears that
of the six capitals which are mentioned in IR only one, financial capital, is
really treated and protected as capital-debt. The other capitals, notably natural capital, appear as simple means (resources in the economic definition,
or assets) and not as debts to be reimbursed, strictly and fully. It is striking,
in this regard, that IR distinguishes "financial capital" and "manufactured
capital". This is not a redundancy. Financial capital is the accounting capital
of capitalists which is a liability, while manufactured capital corresponds
to assets, like the natural and human (social) capitals. For the financial
capital the registration in the balance sheet as a capital means it is to be
strictly conserved. For the two others types of capital some vague information in annexes (reporting) on the way firms endeavour to try to avoid their

destruction: as said by Méda (1999, 61) it means a refusal to their treatment as true patrimony[12]. No parity here: the capitalists do not confuse "*les torchons* (dusters) *avec les serviettes* (with napkins)"! Fourthly, these capitals are principally valued in terms of fair value with all the consequences that we have previously mentioned. Lastly and fifthly, the concepts of limits or of zones of limits do not practically appear and are not even hinted to as a possibility of use by the firms. This testifies that the question of the conservation of natural capital is not a key agenda in this view of reporting which is dominated by a financial philosophy. Nothing serious is to be observed from this proposal of reporting to save the planet.[13] On the contrary it is a kind of smoke screen to imagine that capitalists are making endeavours for the sake of it, while going on the traditional capitalist way (see for more details Rambaud and Richard, 2015a). Gleeson-White (2014, 217), albeit globally favourable to this kind of initiative, has the honesty to recognize that it is based on false premises. She says that "there is a logical inconsistency here", integrated reporting is "being practised by an old-paradigm corporation: essentially, one obliged to make a return on financial capital at the cost of the other capitals". But Gleeson-White ignores the capital-debt conception in her comment on the six capitals, a fact which prevents her from having a complete view of the problem and to propose other solutions.

This enumeration of the 12 proposals and criticism of some capitalist misleading solutions ends the theoretical part of our manifest dedicated to the CARE/TDL method. We insist on the fact that these coordinated changes of accounting and governance of firms are much more adapted than the measures generally proposed by the economists to cope with today's situation. With these solutions of mainstream economists, we are wasting precious time. We will now propose some concrete examples of the application of the CARE/TDL method.

Notes

1 See his interview "Tsunami financier, désastre humanitaire?" www.thinkerview. com.
2 See the declarations of numerous economists and politics in Le Monde of 22/10/1019: "Is finance able to save the world?" (16–17).
3 This does not mean that the consumers do not have a say in the matter (see further in this section).
4 See also the works of Spash, notably his recent article of 2020.
5 We give here only broad principles. For a detailed analysis of the problem see Chenet and Rambaud (2020).
6 In a famous article Costanza et al. (1997) show the interest of having an estimation of the value of the services rendered by the ecosystems; this will allow for people to be more sensitive to the ecological question. As most economists, their valuation relies on prices. But, as is frequently the case for environmental

services such as pure air, there is no market price. Hence they have recourse to fictitious prices obtained by asking people how much they will accept to pay for this kind of service. Generally this type of literature is quoted in the articles devoted to the payments of ecoservices (Wunder, 2005).

7 Most of the time the payments only concern the price paid for the measures to recover the services of the nature, not for the value of the services themselves.

8 We do not speak here of special legal or judicial problems such as the conformity of these agreements with the WTO or the transformation of the traditional property law with special devices such as conventional easements (servitudes), or even the foundation of a new concept of patrimony such as natural patrimony assorted with specific environmental constraints.

9 If we extend this reasoning, all the people who care for their garden or their house could also ask for compensation.

10 See Richard, Bensadon and Rambaud (2018) chapter 18, notably page 308.

11 See for more details De Villiers et al. (2014).

12 One of the frequent justifications for this kind of disparity is that it is difficult to value the human and the natural capitals and that it could be immoral to give them a price. In the best case this type of argumentation, inspired by a capitalist view of the question, emanates from people who have not understood that the conservation of the natural and the human capitals is not an affair of prices but of costs. In the worst case it comes from people who themselves practice the merchandization of these capitals!

13 In the same sense Flower (2015).

3 Application of the CARE/ TDL model at micro and macro levels

Toward a new national system of accounts

We will begin to treat the case of a firm, within the field of micro-economics. After that, on this basis, we extend the treatment to the case of macro-economics. We will then show what could be the solution to a drastic reform of the concept of the Gross Domestic Product (GDP) and the whole of the system of taxation. We thus demonstrate that this concept and, more largely, all of today's national accounting systems are typical instruments to the service of capitalism and totally unfitted to a human and ecological society. We will also indicate the means to replace them on the basis of the CARE/TDL model.

3–1 The application of the CARE/TDL model to business micro accounting systems (firms)

In order to avoid additional effort on behalf of the reader we will use the example of Datini's statements, which have served us as the basis to explain capitalist accounting. We will show how we modify this type of accounting to transform it into an ecological and human accounting. To this goal we introduce two supplementary data issued from the ontological and human analyses of the human and the natural capitals used by Datini. The first is that, to get their full conservation (decent or good life), the employees of Datini should have received a global pay of 120 instead of 50. The second is that Datini should provide a supplementary budget of costs of 40 in order to rent a new ecological tool which will permit the prevention of pollution of the river next to the firm at the time of the manipulation of the merchandises. On the basis of these two types of data we can now reconstruct this *initial balance sheet* to transform it into a balance sheet corresponding to the CARE/TDL philosophy.

In concordance with the axioms of the CARE/TDL model three types of capital now appear under three separate lines on the liabilities' side in the form of budgeted costs. Corresponding to them three lines of assets appear

DOI: 10.4324/9781003194149-5

Table 3.1 Assets Initial Balance sheet, Firm X (CARE/TDL)
Liabilities

Cash (CU)	100	Financial capital	100
Employees (CU)	120	Human capital	120
Natural asset (CU)	40	Natural capital	40

Table 3.2 Assets BS Firm X (CARE/TDL) after the sale
Liabilities

Financial asset (CU)	100-100 0	Financial capital	100
Employees (CU)	120-120 0	Human capital	120
Natural asset (CU)	40-40 0	Natural capital	40
Common cash	300	Common profit	40

on the assets' side, more exactly three different lines of costs of usage (CU) of assets. In this simplified example, which concerns *only one period of activity for the sake of simplification*, all budgets (capitals) represent costs which must be expended within this short period of time[1] in order to maintain all three capitals. After the foundation of the firm, at the time of the next operation, the purchase of wares, this balance sheet will not be fundamentally changed: the cost of the wares purchased will only replace the cash on the asset side. We will pass this operation and see directly the balance sheet after the sale of the wares and the receipt of the corresponding cash but before any new purchase of wares and any payment of the employees or payment for the rent of the ecological tool.

As it appears, in the frame of this human and ecological accounting, the net profit, which is now a common profit of the three capitals, has been reduced: it has decreased from 150 to only 40. It is obviously caused by the fact that the firm, in order to conserve human and natural capital, has been obliged to take account of supplementary expenses of 70 for human capital and 40 for natural capital. Other information, which is also immediately visible on the balance sheet, is that, despite a sufficient amount of "common cash" on the assets side, the firm has not yet taken measures to ensure the conservation of the three capitals. It follows that the three types of capital have been used up without being renewed. Hence the stock of wares is nil. In the same way personnel have been used without receiving any compensation. Finally, we can also see that the firm has not paid the service to clean the river; it cannot be said that it has totally respected its obligation in this matter. Thus, all the corresponding assets have been depreciated and their amounts have been reduced to nil. In a classical way the depreciations of the assets will have as consequence the registration of expenses in the P&L statement. This is shown in the following account:

P&L account Datini
Revenues (common sales)   + 300
Financial depreciation expenses (cost of wares)   -100
Human depreciation expenses (cost of use of employees) -120
Natural depreciation expenses (cost of use of the river) -40
Net common profit   40

We can thus see the appearance of a Triple Depreciation Line (TDL) which permits an estimation of the real global costs of the period corresponding to the conservation of the three capitals. Passet, this visionary economist, lamented that "only the financial capital will be classified with a depreciation which can permit its renewing" (1979, 41). Kapp (1963), this other remarkable exception among economists, proposed that whales ought to be protected via systemic depreciation rules. All these wishes are satisfied with the CARE/TDL method. Of course, each of the three lines of depreciation is composed of many items. More importantly, we can notice that, now, in this new kind of accounting, each capital has its own expenses, as it is notably the case for the employees who are no longer an expense of the financial capital. Now the balance of the P&L statement indicates a true profit after the strict conservation (preservation) of the three capitals. This profit is no longer one of only financial capital. It is considered the result of the action of the three capitals and, hence, as a common profit to them, a profit for three "commoners". E Ostrom (1990) has dreamt of a generalization of the system of commons. The CARE/TDL model offers the basis for this generalization, at the global level, with a new system of accounts capable to replace the IFRS (see the next section). But let us come back to this new kind of human and ecological profit. We see now how fictitious the type of profit derived from the capitalist type of accounting of Datini was. More generally we can say that today the majority of the profits distributed by capitalist firms are fictitious profits, particularly those of the big firms which dominate the economy and force people at a global level into an inhuman and anti-economic competition. In our example of Datini, it is already the case: he has a fictitious profit of 110. Thus, the CARE/TDL accounting can give useful information on the existence of extra-profits in the accounts of financial capitalists. In this regard it can be the basis of a new policy of taxation in favour of human and ecological causes. These extra profits could be entirely taxed and the product of this taxation could be used to give subsidies to the firms which have bigger costs due to their ecological and human policies. These supplementary costs would be also easily detected in the frame of the CARE/TDL model. This could be particularly the case in the frame of agricultural activity. It would give the possibility to the States to encourage those farmers who try to engage in eco-friendly agriculture while taxing the firms which destroy nature, notably those which practice the monoculture associated with the use of pesticides. The profits of supermarkets who do not pay labourers at the fair price, covering their costs corresponding to their conservation, could also be easily identified and taxed. Jouzel and Larrouturou (2019, 296) propose to finance the conversion of the European Union to ecology thanks to a supplementary tax on the benefits of firms. This proposal could be ineffective and even very dangerous if not assorted with specific measures of control. The CARE/TDL method could avoid the *indifferent* treatment of firms which make endeavours for the climate and those which continue their business as usual. The CARE/TDL model should be the basis for such grants. It will permit giving grants only to the firms which make real endeavours in favour of the ecological and human causes and to tax the fictitious profit of the firms which refuse to engage in this way.[2] *It could also be used to tax the importation of foreign wares produced to the detriment of men and nature.* Let us now finish our example by assuming that the firm executes the last step which leads to the conservation of the three capitals. We admit that it uses the amount available in cash for that use. Here is the final balances sheet after this last operation:

Table 3.3 Assets Final BS Firm X (CARE/TDL) Liabilities

Financial asset (CU)	100–100 +100 100		Financial capital	100
Employees (CU)	120–120 +120 120		Human capital	120
Natural asset (CU)	40-40 +40 40		Natural capital	40
Common cash		40	Common net profit	40

What has happened? It is clear that the cash in common has decreased from 300 to 40, which implies a global cash outflow of 260. We can easily see the use of this sum by regarding the evolution of the other lines of assets. We can see that the financial asset has increased by 100. This corresponds to the purchase of a new ware which permits the renewal of financial capital. We also see that the human asset has raised by 120: this corresponds to the impact of the pay for their conservation received by the employees. At last the rented natural asset has also increased by 40. It is the consequence of the payment made for preventing the pollution of the river. We now see that all capitals have been conserved, if we neglect the unavoidable entropy. This state of conservation can immediately be seen by comparing the level of "value" (expressed in conservation costs) of the assets with the amount to be conserved in the liabilities' side of the balance sheet. Normally three types of specialized auditors should certify the reality of this conservation.

All these new types of calculations will consequently have new concepts of return, efficiency and competitiveness which is not possible to study in this book. Let us only repeat that it is an error to speak *in general* of technical rationality or of economic rationality as proposed, notably, by the German school of philosophy: each rationality is conditioned by subjective choices that can be very diverse. We have thus ended with this part devoted to the illustration of the application of the CARE/TDL model to private (or public) firms. But we have underlined that we also want to show how the CARE/TDL model will let "revolutionize" the national accounting systems and, notably, to replace the famous GDP by a new synthetic monetary indicator adapted to ecological and human objectives.

3–2   The application of the CARE/TDL model to macro-accounting: toward a reform of GDP

National accounting has generally been tasked to give an idea on the creation of wealth in a country for a given period of time. Its most well-known indicator is the famous GDP (Gross Domestic Product) although logically the NDP (Net Domestic Product) should be privileged, taking into account the depreciation of fixed assets (like the machines), and, more generally, the depreciation of all assets which serve production over more than one period. Here we will give priority to the latter indicator. Fundamentally, in all countries, the NDP results from the aggregation of micro-economic data mainly furnished by the firms of the country. More precisely it is often only the aggregation of the P&L accounts of the firms, as far as systems of national accounts are rarely in a position to give a national balance sheet. To understand the preparation of these national P&L statements we will take a very simple example inspired by our past reflections over the accounting document of Datini. We first remind you of the P&L statement of this capitalist for the period previously examined, *according to the traditional capitalist method*:

> Revenues (sales) + 300
> Financial depreciation expenses (cost of wares) -100
> Human expenses (cost of use of employees) -50
> Net profit 150

Let us imagine now, for the sake of an outrageous simplification, that this Spanish subsidiary of Datini is an enormous firm which represents the whole of the firms that are active in Spain.[3] Let us also admit that it only has for activity the import and export of wares. Let us suppose that it has imported different wares from abroad for a global amount of 100 to re-sell them in Spain and in other countries for 300. What would be its NDP for the period according to the *classical rules of national accounting without recourse to the TDL method*? Two different methods can be used. The first one is said to be the "deductive approach". It consists of taking the revenues of the period and deducing the necessary consumption of the tools or the materials for the production and the sale of this period. This will allow them to obtain what is called "added value" by the activity of the nation. In our example the product is confounded with the sales. Hence the revenues are represented by the sales. And the consumption is represented by the cost of the wares sold: this consumption is generally called "intermediary consumption" or "depreciation" (in the case of equipment). The *classical capitalist NDP* of this nation is here (in this simplified example) equal to 300 (sales) less 100 (cost of goods sold), which is 200. It is the first way to measure the wealth produced in this country for the period considered. But there is another technique to get the same result. It consists of adding the different types of earnings distributed during the period to the population of this country. In our case there are only two social classes to which correspond two types of earnings. The first is the class of capitalists who received the profits and the second the class of the employees who receive the wages. Thus, this calculation consists of adding the profit of Datini of 150 to the real amount of wages of his employees, which is 50. Thanks to that we can find again the traditional NDP of this nation: 200. We can verify this evidence: one cannot distribute more wealth than produced, known as added value. But this "finding" is secondary. What is more interesting for our inquiry is to compare the micro-economic view given by private accounting of Datini with the macro-economic view of national accounting. We can see that when the micro accounting of Datini has a focus on his profit of 150, the macro national accounting has an interest for the whole of revenues of the nation: it mixes the earnings of the capitalist with those of the wage-owners and gives an indication of their global wealth as if they were a unity with a global earning of 200. In a certain sense J.B. Say would assert that national income is nothing but the sum of the "profits" of the salaried people and of their bosses, the capitalists, all taken on an equal footing. This kind of macro-economic reasoning can be represented by the following P&L statement elaborated on the basis of the first method:

National P&L statement (period x)
Revenue (selling price of the wares sold) + 300
Expense (cost of purchase of the wares sold) -100
Balance ("national global profit" or NDP) = 200

Let us underline that today this kind of macro-economic measure is published in practically all countries of the world and that economists generally

take it as the basis of their judgment of the evolution of the economic performance at the national and even of the global level: it is the indicator
which dominates today's macro-economic thought. In light of this account
the reader could think that, as far as it is concerned a macro-economic datum
(the added value, derived from the joint (common) action (work) of the
capitalists and their employees), this kind of national statement could offer
a *more neutral conception* of accounting than the private P&L statement of
Datini which only shows its private benefit. In fact, contrary to all appear-
ances, this is not the case, as we will show. Thanks to the preceding developments dedicated to the CARE/TDL model, the reader already knows that
the figures of wages and profits of capitalist accounting do not give a true
and fair view of the earnings of the firm. Indeed, they do not take account
of the true cost of human capital and of natural capital. This observation,
relative to the private accounts of Datini, is also true for the case of national
accounts: the latter are based on the accounts of capitalist firms. Thus all
of today's national accounts give an incorrect view of the performance of
nations. We will confirm this assertion by showing what should be the correct national accounting in the case of the Datini's subsidiary in Spain. In
order to do that we will start from the *correct P&L statement of Datini* as
established according to the rules of the CARE/TDL method:

Revenue (sales)	+ 300
Financial depreciation expense (cost of purchase of goods sold)	-100
Human depreciation expense (cost of use)	-120
Ecological depreciation expense (cost of use)	-40
Net common profit	= 40

On this basis we can now resume our calculation of the NDP of Spain to take
account of the real amount of the depreciation of all the types of capitals and
finally arrive at a correct NDP. Again, we can distinguish the deductive and
the additive method. According to the deductive method we deduct all the
expenses of consumption of the different capitals (260) from the revenue of
the sales (300), and we get an NDP of only 40. Why this enormous difference with the official NDP of 200? Because, contrary to the capitalist view,
in order to get the *true added value*, we are obliged to consider that there are
three lines of depreciation corresponding to the conservation of three types
of capitals and not only one. Hence the global amount of the depreciation
expense is not 100, as it is the case with the capitalist national accounting,
but 260. With this type of reasoning the NDP of 40 will be confused with
the common profit of the CARE/TDL method, reflecting the true and correct
profit of the firm Datini, as well as Spain. Such is the true measure of the
creation of wealth of a nation, calculated at the macro-economic level on

the basis of "sane" micro economic data, notably a correct interpretation of the *concept of conservation* of the three types of capitals. This will permit at last to conceive an ecological NDP: the CARE/TDL NDP. It will cause a revolution in National Accounting.

We have thus demonstrated that today's national accounting systems give a totally biased view of the wealth of nations and of the economic performance because they are totally inspired by a capitalist conception of capital. They are also instruments at the service of capitalists. To get out of this situation it is necessary to rely on a new type of accounting such as the CARE/TDL model. The conclusion is obvious: we must first change the accounting system of firms, which is at the basis of any system of national accounts. But this will not be possible without a radical transformation of the governance of firms and of companies' law. This leads us to our next part.

Notes

1 We underline once more that the choice of a short and unique period is made for practical reasons. The budgets may concern longer periods depending on the horizon of time of the members of the firm.

2 Moreover the control of the reality of the endeavours of the firms could be better realized in the frame of the co-management conceived along the CARE/TDL method than in the frame of today's capitalist governance of firms, as shown by Foucart, on the basis of an inquiry made by *The New York Times*, (Le Monde 5–6 Janvier 2020, 24: "Une catastrophe agricole commune") the European subsidies to the agriculture have up to now mainly benefited big firms that do not respect the conservation of the environment.

3 As Jouvenel (1968) said, national accounting is based on private accounting.

Part II

Toward a new governance of firms and nations

Introduction

Any accounting system is dominated by a subject who imprints the mark of his power on it (Richard et al., 2018, 14). As shown by Perez (2003), this power is the main characteristic of any type of governance, notably of firms. In the accounting model inherited from capitalist merchants and industrials of the 13th and 14th centuries there has always been only one type of capital to be protected on the liabilities' side of the balance sheet: financial capital. The other types of capital, natural and human capital, have been treated as mere assets to be used. Today's capitalist accounting law continues to perpetrate the sole protection of the financial and even, with the imprudent IFRS, to reinforce it to the detriment of the other types of capital. But this kind of law is not the only one that capitalists "obey". It is accompanied, notably, by companies' law and, more largely, by the enterprise's law when it exists. Companies' law, which is the matrix of accounting law, does not only oblige to treat solely financial capital as a debt to be reimbursed: *it also gives to this type of capital the monopoly of power inside the company*. Thus, generally, practically in all countries of the world, today's system of law, which is so proud of justice (*Jus est ars boni et aequi*), has never put the three main capitals which form the basis of any firm on an equal footing. It admits the absolute reign of capitalists in the firm everywhere. At best, in countries that have social democrats in power, it tries to limit the damages caused by the capitalist system, notably thanks to labour laws and faltering environmental laws. In the following lines we will only discuss companies' law, more precisely of its part that concerns Joint Stock companies. We will concentrate our analysis and our proposal of reforms on these monsters of capitalism which dominate the scene today (and not on small and medium enterprises). We must first mention that, since the World War I, a certain number of courageous lawyers, and even some very rare captains of industries like Rathenau (1917), have tried to change or to amend capitalist

DOI: 10.4324/9781003194149-6

society through proposals of reforms of companies' law. These were first and chiefly German lawyers (see further in this chapter), followed by French and American ones.[1] All of them have tried to think about a new conception of the big firm which could, notably, make it a "firm as itself" (in German an "Unternehmen an sich"). This kind of new firm would be prized with a more or less public objective, which will avoid capitalists, notably absent owners or shareholders, dominating the scene to the detriment of wage labourers or of employees and, more largely, of the simple creditors and, even long-term thinking, shareholders. We have no place here to analyze in detail their interesting work. We will only quote the names of some of them like Rathenau (1917), Friedländer (1927), Geiler (1927), Haussmann (1928), Netter (1929), Passow (1930), all German, then Dodd (1932), Percerou (1932), Berle and Means (1932), Ripert (1946), Durand (1947), Berle (1954), Despax (1957), Champaud (1962), Paillusseau (1967) and Contin (1975). In France, this type of thought, initiated by Percerou (1932) and Ripert (1946), has later taken the name of "economic doctrine of the enterprise" with, notably, Champaud (1962). This current of ideas has had an eclipse in the years between 1995 and 2008, at the time of the rise of the "Friedmanian" ideology (see the next section) but has seen a certain renaissance after the economic crisis of 2008. For example, Champaud, in two recent writings published under his direction, deems that, to cope with financial capitalism, it is necessary to "give back economic power to the undertakers (2011, 223). He also asserts that the economic doctrine of the enterprise is "fundamentally in homothety" with the theses of the American Stakeholders Theory (AST) (Champaud, 2011, 219). This American theory can be considered as a modern resurgence of the old German "Unternehmen an sich" which was developed before World War II by initiators like Geiler, Haussmann and Netter. One of its main founders is Freeman (1984). His main idea, which is not a novelty (see our Volume 1), is that it is the task of enlightened managers to instore within the firm a dialog with (and between) the so called "stakeholders" (practically employees, creditors, shareholders and consumers) to conciliate their diverging interests with the interest of the firm (see for more details Richard, 2012a, 2015a, 2016). It is clear that his idea relies on the managerialist conception of the firm developed by Berle and Means in 1932. As we have seen, according to this view, the managers of big firms with numerous small shareholders are reputed to have the power and thus be able to reunify the different interests under their umbrella: they control the firm. This modern AST inspires today a lot of works of numerous progressivist lawyers which are fundamentally in accordance with the idea that the social interest of the firm cannot be assimilated with the interest of the sole shareholders, more particularly short-term oriented shareholders. It is the case, among them, of diverse authors like (in alphabetical order) Abadie (2013), Bezard (2004), Daigre (1996), Teller (2011), Teyssié (2004), Tchotourian (2010, 2013), Trébulle (2006a, 2006b, 2007a, 2007b), in France, Rousseau and Tchotourian (2009) in Canada and France, Blair (1994), Blair and Stout (1999), Greenfield (2006), and Stout (2012) in the US. They all are inspired, directly or indirectly, and to a diverse extent, by the old theses of the German founders of the "Unternehmen an sich" or of the French "doctrine de l'entreprise", reviewed by the American AST. All these authors form an influential (but not dominant) stream which tries to struggle against the "mainstream". The latter is represented by ancient lawyers like Labbé, as early as 1883, and much later, by the famous and mighty American school of the "Economics of law" animated, notably, in the US, by lawyers such as Bainbridge (1993), Hansmann and Kraakman (2000), Romano (2001), and, in France, by Martin (2005), Mestre (1989) and Mathey (2001). All these authors defend a contractual view of the firm, not an institutional view. It is clear that today these are the lawyers of the mainstream who dominate the scene at the global level and support, in a very efficient way, financial capitalism. The lawyers of the "small stream" who defend the old idea of the "firm as itself" (or the firm as an entity) have enormous difficulties to impose their views. This is what some members of this "small stream" like Rousseau and Tchotourian (2009) openly recognize. Their difficulties come from different reasons. Firstly, as seems to be the case in all countries, the recourse to the concept of "social interest" or (interest of the firm), even if it is evoked in certain texts of law or by the jurisprudence, is generally a fuzzy one. For lack of precision it is entirely left to the disposition of the managers supposed to use it. Most of the time a typically fuzzy phrase in the texts mentions that the administrators or the directors "may take account (or at best should take account) of other interests as those of the shareholders". It is clear for us that this absence of strict obligation is in conformity with the philosophy of the AST that has confidence in the spirit of responsibility of the enlightened managers. The consequence is a considerable margin of action for these managers: all will depend on their good will. Secondly, in the majority of cases, neither the laws nor the jurisprudence give a clear definition of the "stakeholders". Again this other type of fuzziness reinforces the possibilities of maneuver of the managers. Thirdly, even in rare cases when there is a will to give some precision on the concepts of social interest and of stakeholders there remain difficulties, nevertheless. As showed, notably by Rousseau and Tchotourian (2009), the result is most of the time deceitful. The main cause is a lack of instruments of economic and accounting management to permit an application of the general rules. The main questions are: who are the stakeholders and what are their legitimated interests? How to measure the equilibrium between these diverse interests? What are the means to value these interests? What is the concept of profit which corresponds to the conception of the social interest of the firm? As many questions to which the AST has been unable to respond clearly and give a practical basis. Moreover, as we showed in Volume 1, the managerial thesis of Berle and Means, which serves as a basis of the AST, is not funded; the managers of the capitalist firm are not neutral persons but well paid allies of the capitalists, if not simple "clerks", in the Smithian sense. The conclusion to be drawn from all these elements is clear: a new law based on the concepts and proposals of AST is of poor usefulness to find a way to build a new type of ecological and human governance of firms; it cannot cope with the mighty structure and precision of the legal instruments of capitalist governance, notably its accounting devices. This is the reason we propose a recourse to another theory of the governance of the JSC: the "Integral Theory of Capital Holders" (ITCH) or, in French, "Théorie Intégrale des Investisseurs en Capital (TIIC). We think that it is time that human beings who work, and nature which gives its treasures, should be considered as true investors in the same way as financial capitalists. Capitalism has the gift of capturing flattering terms; it has monopolized the term investor, notably in the frame of the IFRS. ITCH will rectify the situation: starting from the principle of equality of the three capitals. But it does not limit itself to the enunciation of beautiful principles. In contrast with AST it relies on an accounting model, the CARE/TDL accounting model. We will now present its axiomatic in the matter of governance of firms then show how it differs from other attempts in the same direction. We will then specify how these new conceptions of the firm and of a new law on joint-stock companies will be incorporated in the constitutions and permit the rise of a new type of governance of nations.

Note

1 These developments are mainly based on Richard (2016).

4 The axiomatic of a new type of ecological governance of firms

ITCH

These axioms include the necessity of the realization of a just equilibrium between the different capitals invested, the promotion of common values and interests, the redefinition of social interest and the transformation of accounting law.

4–1 The realization of a just equilibrium between different capitals

As shown previously a group of progressive lawyers has, for many years, tried to modify companies' law to provide more justice to different types of investors. Their goal was to establish an "equilibrium" or a balance or, even, for some of them, a "community" of interests (Rousseau and Tchotourian, 2009, 3). We think that such a balance can be achieved through the incorporation of ITCH into corporate law. This incorporation should comprise three main items. Firstly, the reminder that there are three main types of capital to be preserved (conserved) on the liabilities' side of the balance sheet. This is the integration at the corporate law level of the basic axiom of the CARE/ TDL method. Secondly, the enunciation that these capitals will be classified with an equal participation to the governance of the JSC (or the firm). In the model of companies' laws inherited from capitalist company law, only the representatives of financial capital have the right to name administrators and to take the most important decisions concerning the life of the JSC. In the new company law in line with ITCH, this right will be recognized for the representatives of the three main capitals. It has been shown that, in this regard, two main solutions may compete (Richard, 2012). The first one is that of "ecological capitalism". It is a kind of extension of the rule of financial capitalism. It consists of granting the rights to vote to the representatives of the three capitals in proportion of their relative amount of capital as it appears on the liabilities' side of the balance sheet. Although

DOI: 10.4324/9781003194149-7

this solution seems to be possible, we have rejected it on behalf of technical problems (complexity of the day-to-day variation of these capitals) and, foremost, of deontological problems: why, for example, should the relative importance of human capital (in the sense of CARE) justify the degree of participation of the persons in the decisions of the firm if we assume that every human being is an autonomous person with equal right of participation in the affairs of the city in the larger sense (including the firms inside this city)? The second solution is to promote what we call a new "ecological co-management" (ECM). In the frame of this solution each type of capital will have one third of the global voting power to be shared on strict parity among the different representatives of these capitals, independently of the size of their investment as represented in the liabilities' side of the CARE/ TDL balance sheet. We make two preliminary remarks on this choice of the ECM. The first is that it is not detrimental to financial investors in the eyes of today's dominant view of the problem. Indeed studies (notably that of the World Bank, 2006) show that the size of human capital is largely superior to that of financial capital. The second is that the size of capital invested is taken into account at the level of the conservation of the capitals but plays, on the contrary, no role in the matter of participation in the decisions. In a sense we come back to the initial stage of familial capitalism when all members of the family, at least male members, were associated in a spirit of parity along the principle of one woman/man one voice; we speak of a familial view of the companies at the world level (the human world family). Concerning the question of the nomination of the representatives of the three types of capitals, we will limit ourselves to broad remarks. The representatives of financial capital will not only be composed of traditional shareholders, but also that of creditors and of the mass of suppliers: all those who invest tangible or intangible financial means into the firm, including the States and the tribes which allow for soils, for example. We have already stressed that in the frame of the new type of society which will emerge with ITCH and the development at the world level of new types of workers cooperatives, there will be a new type of financial investor very different from the today's, even more that this type of investor will no longer have a power based on the importance of its stake. The representatives of human capital will be directly nominated by employees themselves who work for the company on the basis of clear mandates. Trade unions will not be represented in this type of co-management. But they will conserve their traditional role of defenders of employees and have a new important role to play in the matter of definition of the ontology of human capital (see the previous section). They will also have an important role in the contestation of the new system of management, a case which is not compatible with their participation into its management. This is one of the differences with the famous German co-determination among others (see the next section). Finally the representatives of natural capital will be, notably, scientific independent experts (like member of the GIEC, agronomists, ecologists. . .), but also members of independent NGOs, *residents* concerned by the actions of the firm,[1] and also staff members who have a particular knowledge of these problems and have proven their interest for ecological questions. It thus appears that workers or former workers can intervene within the framework of this co-management at the level of representation of the three types of capital while specifying that they cannot sit in the three groups of representatives at the same time.

All these representatives will act not only at the level of the Board or of a specialized council of surveillance, as is the case in traditional experiences of co-management, but also at the level of the directors and the main stages of the whole structure of the company, notably the divisions and the workshops. On the whole, this new co-management appears as a true and wide participation model that some scholars like Blair (1994), Stout (2012), L. Sève and J. Sève (2018[2]) have wanted. But, to the difference of the latter, it is an *institutionalized* co-management *guaranteed* by a profound modification of companies' and accounting laws. All that is very different from the German co-determination, all the more than the latter gives no possibility for a true ecological representation. This solution is also very different from the American Stock Holder Theory. Indeed, according to ITCH, only the investors of the three types of capital of the CARE/TDL model are members of the ecological co-management, which allows the clear definition and delimitation of the stakeholders who have power. This obviously does not prevent a consultation of other stakeholders such as clients,[3] the public, other firms, etc. which will be represented in ad hoc commissions. Thus, we have here a "Capital Holder Theory" at the very basis of the whole system, based on a complete accounting system encompassing a redefinition of the concept of profit, which is impossible in the frame of the AST. This leads us to the following point.

4–2 The promotion of common values and interests with a new concept of common profit

In the CARE/TDL model a new concept of profit appears: it is obtained after the registration of a triple depreciation line, which allows for the conservation (preservation) of three capitals. It is based on a true full cost which normally permits the preservation of ecosystems and of all employees. In the frame of this new model of society we make the hypothesis that all financial capitalists became either active persons in firms who benefit of this type of protection, or pensioned people who also benefit of the same preservation. These new financial investors thus no longer have the necessity to live on the basis of a financial capital, of financial rents and may be, for the ecological firms, the source of a private financing of a new kind, very different from today's situation. This hypothesis is important because it relies on the principle that, in this new conception of the firm, any systematic and regular distribution of dividends is excluded. This is a kind of return to the very ancient position of the Christian Church, even an extension of it[4]. This position could appear as totally unrealistic to the defenders of today's capitalist system. But, as far as the lenders of money are concerned, the history of capitalism proves that it is perfectly possible to compel these lenders to be totally deprived of any systematic interest (see the next section). Thus the "fate" of the new profit will depend on the common decision of the three types of new investors, more exactly of their representatives. The latter, as they manage a common profit, become true associated people for better or worse, which will normally make them possible allied partners and not, as it is the case today, in capitalist accounting, systematic adversaries. As in any classical JSC, this common profit is a testament to good management and its use will be freely determined by the annual general assembly of the new partners. Normally, the fact that the employees and the new financial investors are assured of the conservation (preservation) of their stakes should motivate them to treat these profits as retained earnings for the self-financing of the future expansion of their firm or the betterment of the natural capital (reparation of environmental functions degraded in the past, betterment of the quality of the soils beyond the limits to be observed, etc.). If necessary, to foster self-financing, it would be possible to renew with the old rule of the "two-fold 50%" of the prudent "classical" finance which existed before their demolition by the so called "modern" finance: the obligation to put in retained earnings at least 50% of the annual profit and obligation to have a minimum of equity of 50% in the liabilities' side of the balance sheet. However, distributions of dividends (in the new sense of this term) are possible, if justified, case by case. It may notably (not exclusively) concern outlays for the investors of the human capital or who cope with particularly difficult or important tasks: they will receive, beyond the pay for their preservation, an income whose principles will be decided by the representatives of the human capital.[5] We still insist in this regard that these payments are a real income, the retention of the workers concerned having been made beforehand during the payment of a correct pay. Secondly, other casual outlays may be made in favour of the (new) financial capitalists for their strategic or long-term investments. We speak of "new financial investors" animated with another spirit than that of today's capitalist shareholders: they could notably be former retired workers who would be pleased to invest in the new type of ecological and human companies. In any case the association of a very large number of employees to the fate of their company should normally permit them to get out of their situation of feeling alienated: they also will be considered as true investors[6]! The betterment of their situation will be all the more important if measures of *fragmentation* of the big international monsters are taken to transform them into companies with a human size. This question of firm size comes up more and more often in the past and present context of the development of supermarkets and large online retailers such as Amazon. These trade giants are increasingly accused of having contributed to the destruction of small businesses in towns as well as to a dehumanization of trade relations: instead of being able to meet human beings who serve them close to their home, people, especially in small towns, have to travel by car to increasingly automated supermarkets or have to shop online. This question of the "dehumanization" of commercial relations typically arises from a choice of society and preservation of (societal) capital which must be decided on democratically. The citizens of each state should be consulted on this point and, if necessary, if they prefer to return to forms of commerce which allow more human relations, ask these states to take measures to force the large commercial firms to open systematically small stores in town centres managed within the framework of ecological and human co-management of the type of the CARE/TDL model. Of course, this breakthrough of the co-management at both firm and state level (see the next section), will be interpreted by some Marxists as a new attempt to bring alive the old idea of collaboration of the capital and the work force. But, beyond the fact that the protection of the capitals and the distribution of power are drastically changed, it remains that trade unions are totally free to contest this new system. We note that, in France, even such old adversaries of the co-management like the French CGT (Confédération Générale du Travail) admit now that their representatives could participate in the organs of the capitalist firms; if it is already the case in the frame of a pure financial capitalism, it seems to be also possible in the frame of our new kind of society which gives real power of decision to the employees. All the more that the establishment of the new ecological co-management and the suppression of the wage worker condition do not imply the disappearance of the labour law to which the trade unions will continue to contribute: one must not confuse wage labourers and labourers!

4–3 The redefinition of the company and of its social interest

With ITCH and the CARE/TDL method it is no longer possible to consider that the "capitals" are limited to those invested by shareholders. The new kind of society which we promote is a "tri-capitalist" society which associates all the investors of Natural Capital, Human Capital and Financial

Capital. On this basis it seems possible to redefine the concept of social interest of all these new "capitalists". We underline that we will not try to distinguish between the concepts of "social interest" and "social aim", a distinction which seems to us rather fuzzy. We will consider that the social interest of the new capitalists is double. Firstly, it is to conserve (preserve) their capital, which is a-priori warranted by the use of the CARE/TDL method. We may underline that this systematic conservation of every type of capital is not a banal thing; all the more it must be done in constant purchasing power and take into account the context of the society in which these capitals operate. Every person who has invested in the purchase of a house knows that, if one takes account of the importance of the repairs for this house, the simple fact to be assured of its conservation is already a consider- ⋅ able event. Secondly, their goal, like in the case of any JSC, may be to make profits. But of course, profits of a new type, as defined by the CARE/TDL method. We argue for the rehabilitation of the concept of profit, a term which has been corrupted by financial capitalists. In Latin, language profit means something that will do good for something or someone, such as what we can even today find in the French expression "*profitable pour la santé*" (good for health). Originally, it has not the sense of any exploitation, on the contrary. The CARE/TDL profit is also a good thing because it does not impair the three capitals. This profit, as we have shown, must be considered as a residual amount which testifies of the good management of the three capitals, notably of true economies of costs. Since the preservation (conservation) of the three capitals is obligatory, there is in principle no risk that this search for profit leads to production and consumption harmful to nature. This new kind of profit is freely distributable by the representatives of the three capitals under, eventually, the constraints of the self-financing previously evoked. We underline again that it is a residue in the strictest sense. In ITCH there is no question that any of the new capitalists may require a predetermined interest (or cost of capital in the sense of modern finance), in proportion of his capital. This rule is obvious for the natural "investor" but also applicable to the two other types of investors. This constitutes, as already mentioned, a kind of return to the traditional (and good) position of the Catholic church, before Bernardin de Sienne, at the time when it condemned any form of interest. Let us underline that modern capitalism is able to impose this de facto rule when the banks are obliged by the regulators of the financial markets to lower their interest rates to practically nothing: our solution is thus just the extension and the generalization of this peculiar "capitalist" practice which has dominated the scene in the 19th century (see our Volume 1). Of course, as is in principle the case in the frame of financial capitalism (see further in this chapter for the nuance), if the business turns bad, the new investors must share the losses. In the frame of this new ecological co-management all the investors share the burden of these losses: they are entirely responsible for their actions. But there is not such a big change in comparison with today's situation. Indeed, as more and more people recognize it, the time is long gone when financial capitalists could present themselves as the sole risk takers in the firm, in contrast, as they assert, to the employees. We know that the global evolution of capitalist companies' law has been marked by a progressive reduction of the legal responsibility of financial capitalists, notably in the case of losses. This began in the middle of the 19th century with the passage from an entire, unlimited, legal responsibility to a limited one. We also know, even, that this kind of limited responsibility is often avoided, at least by very big firms, in the case of national and international crises. It suffices to refer to the well-known examples of this kind of mildness from the part of the legal authorities at the time of the 2008 crisis and, more recently, the coronavirus crisis. We also know financial capitalists have the possibility to practice clever financial portfolio management to diversify their risks. They may also play with the famous "leverage effect" to reduce the mass of their invested capital and let the risks fall to the creditors. More recently they have had recourse to the massive weapon of systematic reimbursements of their stakes by the firms to transform their shares into so-called shares of "enjoyment". All the good textbooks of finance describe these classical tools of capitalists to reduce or avoid their financial responsibility. But one of the best insurances for them is to claim the distribution of systematic, massive and regular dividends as it has been the case since the end of the 19th century. Their "climax" is even bigger when these dividends are calculated on the basis of expected costs of capital reaching an amount of 10–15%. In these cases, we can observe, as the stock market press generally indicates it, that these modern capitalists, if they play at middle or long term, are generally winners: they have got the possibility to earn enough dividends during the good years to come out victorious of the affair even in the case of big crises. Let us underline a fundamental supplementary point in the frame of this comparison of the risks of the financial capitalist with those of the wage employees. Since at least the time of J.B. Say it is traditional, in the debates on this question, to put wages and dividends on an equal footing. The wages of the employees would be the income of the human capital like the dividends are the income of capitalists for their financial capital. The problem is that this type of argumentation is totally misguided. The wages, in today's capitalist world, are, generally, not real income: as shown by the CARE/TDL model a pay only constitutes a true income of human capital if it is a supplementary payment after the preservation of this kind of capital. The situation is totally different in the case of dividends distributed to shareholders. They always concern *true revenues* because they are distributed after the systematic conservation of the financial capital.[7] On the contrary, for the great mass of the wage owners, the so-called income (or dividends, to take the appellation used for the shareholders) are not even sufficient to permit the preservation of their human capital, or just sufficient. It is thus absurd to compare dividends and wages under the capitalist realm. It is true that, in the case of the bankruptcy of a firm, we can see situations when the capitalists, often small capitalists, unable to correctly manage their stakes, will lose their stakes, while wage owners, in the same case, could receive unemployment subsidies. But this protection of the salaried people only exists in developed countries and, when it exists, is limited to a short period. Moreover, it generally concerns a pay corresponding to a simple subsistence for people who have no financial capital to live on. The situation is very different in the case of capitalists, even small capitalists, who generally may have received true and massive revenues during the period of their investments and may also have different sources of revenues. To conclude on these points, today's wage owners should not hesitate to want to take the same risks as those which the financial capitalists affirm to endure. They should retake the slogan of these capitalists when they invoke their famous CSR: we also we want to share the same responsibility as you in the firms. Consequently, with ITCH, a "new risk society" will emerge where the three types of capitals will share the same difficulties with the help of the States in the context of crises, as is already the case for financial capitalists, at least the big ones. We will live in a fully responsible collective society which at the same time satisfies the needs of sustainable development and the attraction of profitable activity in the frame of a special type of market economy, which will be socialized through the mechanisms of the general and systematic conservation of all people. Up to this time the discussion between the Marxists and the Capitalists had reduced the economic debate to the restricted choice between capitalist private firms operating in markets regulated by the liberals or the socio-democrats and nationalized organizations regulated by communist bureaucrats in the frame of an authoritarian planning. In the frame of this terrible iron collar we could only go from Charibde to Scilla! ITCH and the CARE/TDL model permit an escape from this yoke, which has prevented us from any real evolution. As Ostrom (1990) has well seen the fundamental question is not that of the type of property (public or private), but that of the type of management. ITCH at last gives to a great mass of citizens the word and the possibility to be responsible for their acts in the firms in the frame of a generalized protection. They will no longer be the victims of a terrible alienation in the frame of capitalism, as in communism. As shown by Joas (1992), as early as the end of the 19th century, there has been an animated discussion of philosophers and sociologists about the possibility to pursue rational ends (notably economic ones) without preventing the creativity of human beings: the majority of these authors have asserted that it is quite impossible. It seems to us that our proposal of the CARE/TDL method shows that this famous and permanent debate is largely devoid of ground. It is perfectly possible to pursue new rational economic and ecologic ends in the frame of a new social system which permits a large liberty of action of people, notably in their workplaces. This, precisely, in the context of ITCH type of governance. But this situation will be impossible without the emergence of new accounting laws, the following and last element of our inquiry on a new governance of firms.

4–4 The institution of new national and international accounting laws

Some specialists of Buddhism, like Rossignol and Vincenti (2019), think that capitalists themselves, convinced by the wise philosophy of Buddha, will revise their values and transform today's financial capitalism into a "compassionate capitalism" which will take care of nature. But, more seriously, many lawyers, notably Delmas-Marty (2013), have underlined that sustainable development will not occur without law.[8] We share this point of view in line with the historical development of humanity: most of human progress has been reached with the help of laws demanded by people. But we add that these laws cannot be only environmental law and companies' law: it must first of all be accounting laws. But, curiously, in almost all the articles dedicated to the question of environmental or corporate laws, the question of accounting law is absent. However, as shown already by Max Weber (1920a, 1920b, 1921) then by René Savatier (1969), the problem of accounting rationality and of its expression in accounting statements is a fundamental one, to begin in the frame of modern capitalism. Ultimately, shareholders judge the performance of the firm on the basis of the accounting data that are communicated to them, more precisely on the basis of the bottom line of the P&L statement. To want a change of companies' law and to only introduce a new concept of social interest without modifying capitalist accounting law is practically void to failure. Even if some so-called enlightened managers or administrators would change the situation they will face the "realities" of accounting law which make capitalist profit the king criteria of management. Or, as shown before, this criterion is a pernicious one. It notably promotes and organizes the struggle of shareholders against wage owners. It is thus totally at odds with the desire of progressive lawyers to conciliate the different interests at stake in firms. The very structure of the capitalist P&L statement, with the presence of wages expenses, makes these expenses a burden for the capitalist. To radically change this situation, it is first of all necessary to change the definition of accounting profit in accounting law which implies a change of the concept of capital. Afterwards, the essential is done. At the limit it is even not necessary to change companies' law. The latter generally makes reference to accounting concepts, notably to that of profit, without giving any precision on its calculation: this task is delegated to accounting legislation. Finally, we see that the precondition for every change of the governance of firms and, more largely, of any reform of economics, lies in the realization of a drastic modification of accounting law.[9] In our time of globalization, it will mean to change the IFRS as adopted by the different states of the world. One possible strategy would be that two or three important (and courageous) states will unite to refuse today's situation, give the good example to other hesitating states and provoke an accounting crisis which will lead to this change. But other solutions are possible. Notably, the chances of change will rise if some important international "advanced, progressive" firms are prepared to experiment with the CARE/TDL method. The chances of this change will be even better if the CARE method could be applied in parallel to the IFRS (see the next chapter).This is the intention of the CARE/TDL method: to permit all these experiences which will lead to the change of capitalist accounting. We will now show its originality by comparing ITCH to other attempts of reforming the capitalist system.

Notes

1 Notably, for example in Brazil, representatives of the tribes which live near firms operating in the Amazonian forests. This new perspective will be a major step for the defence of these tribes against ecological destructions.
2 In their book about "capital exit" these two authors, in spite of their Marxist approach, realistically admit both shareholders and stakeholders take part in the organs of decisions of companies of a new type (2018, 143)
3 The idea of Borrits (2018, 200 and 212) to institute "Councils of orientations" of consumers at the level of the firms in charge of production, at least the big ones, is interesting; we think that it can be applied in the ITCH model of governance.
4 The Deuteronomy xxiii, 21 says: "unto a stranger thou may lend upon usury but unto thy brother thou shall not lend usury". Similar rules can be found in the Koran as shown by El Diwany (2003, 25). But with CARE we treat all the members of the human family in equal terms.
5 We see here that the concept of income is reserved for the pays in excess of the pay for the preservation of human capital. The latter pay is not an income but only corresponds to the pure preservation of capital.
6 This new situation will foster the appearance of a new "race" of financial investors who will be ready to participate in the financing of their firms or other firms on the basis of totally different motivations as the traditional capitalist investors. A true popular capitalism could emerge with the ITCH model.
7 Thus capitalist accountants do treat these two elements differently – wages are an expense to be paid before arriving at profit, whereas dividends to (ordinary) shareholders should only be paid if there is a residual profit.

8 In the same sense Lordon (2019, 258) shows that the strategies of avoidance of political action and of research of the Spinozian beatitude to change the world are void to failure. He justly insists in the necessary transformation of the law, notably the right of property, which does not mean the elimination of private property, even of the means of production.

9 Peyrelevade (2005, 79 and 94) a former big manager of French groups wants the control of all norms by the political power but, unfortunately, does not propose a concrete reform of the accounting standards.

5   The originality of ITCH
Comparison with alternative models

We only treat here of proposals that are comparable to ours, as far as it concerns their philosophies. We begin with the most ancient, that of the Swiss economist Peter Ulrich, unjustly forgotten. Then we discuss more recent proposals: the American lawyer Greenfield, John Ikerd and, in France (or in French language), Bachet, the Circle of the Bernardins, Isabelle Ferreras, Swann Bommier and Cécile Renouard and, to finish, Thomas Piketty.

5–1 The new society of Peter Ulrich

Peter Ulrich, as early as 1977, rejects the American managerial theses according to which power has passed into the hands of a technocratic elite and asserts that shareholders continue to exercise their domination in firms. He draws the conclusion that it is not possible to rely on the managerial class to reform capitalist management. He deems that only the recourse to drastic laws modifying the nature of power inside the central organs of JSC will permit that. He wants to instore the pluralism at the heart of big firms. He proposes that Boards will be composed of 30% of representatives of the financial capital, 10% of managers, 30% of employees and 30% of representatives of the public sphere (notably of commissions designed by the State regrouping independent experts and scientists). His stakeholder type of proposal, institutionalized by laws, is far ahead of his time. It comes well before that of Freeman and is much more audacious. As many non-American attempts, it has been unjustly forgotten. Despite its quality it lacks reform proposals for accounting laws, which makes it fragile, and does not take an ecological stance. These are the main differences with ITCH.

5–2 The new society of Greenfield

Contrary to his colleagues Blair and Stout, Greenfield (2006), like Ulrich, does not believe that the American companies' law protects the firms

DOI: 10.4324/9781003194149-8

against shareholder value and contests the fact that the managers could play a role of impartial referees between the different interests. Thus, he wants to impose by law a drastic reform of American companies' law to modify the power inside the Boards and institute a true "stakeholder governance". He also deems necessary a fundamental reform of the concept of profit, which is rare in the American context. But he adds that this reform has to objectively take into account the "social and environmental externalities". This last point, as shown before, is problematic, as denoting a neo-classic stance. Another problem is that his interesting proposals are not followed by concrete means of application, notably in the field of accounting.

5–3 The sustainable capitalism of John Ikerd

This American agricultural economist considers that "ecological integrity and social equity must be imposed upon the capitalist economy from the outside by society through public policies to ensure that the economy functions for the long-term benefits of society" (1). He stresses that "the firm belief system must be expressed . . . within the ethical and social context of sustainability" and wishes a return to "the principles of classical capitalism" (77). He makes a severe criticism of the economics of maximizing wealth (19) and also of the ecological economics based on the theory of internalizing externalities with the help of discount rates (67–69). We agree with all these considerations. The problem here is with the means to realize these objectives. Ikerd believes that it could be sufficient to oblige the firms to respect constitutional commitments (118) and that the government "insure the competitiveness of markets" (186). We think that these good wishes cannot be realized without the transformation of the capitalist accounting system, a question which Ikerd does not consider.

5–4 The dualistic structure of Daniel Bachet

Daniel Bachet (2007, 210–212), in an original and profound survey, proposes to legally organize the "confrontation" of the conception on the firm between the salaried workers and the shareholders. For that purpose, he proposes instituting two kinds of organisms with two types of criteria of management. Firstly, there is a Board of Administration where the shareholders will (as it seems) conserve the majority of the power despite the presence of a certain proportion of representatives of the wage owners; this organ will appreciate the performance of the firm from the point of view of the traditional criteria of (capitalist) profit. Secondly, he institutes a "Council of the firm as an entity" whose goal is to permit the reunion (the meeting) of the collective of employees. At this level the criteria of management will be not the profit but, as suggested by Brodier (2001), an indicator of added value of the type used in macroeconomic accounting for the calculation of the GDP and the NDP. According to this system the directors and the managers of the firm will have to act by taking into account these two different views. They will receive their legitimacy of two different organs recognized by the companies' laws. This proposal deals with a kind of institutionalization of the traditional conflict, which exists in firms. The problem with that ingenious construction is that, in our view, it leaves to the managers, always nominated by the shareholders, the role of arbiters without clear accounting constraints. Furthermore, the ecological question is not really treated. But in a recent book (2019) Bachet enlarges his conception by favouring an interesting approach which would incorporate the accounting solutions proposed by the CARE/TDL model, a model to which he explicitly refers (2019, 70–82).

5–5   The Company with Extended Social Object (CESO) proposed by the Circle of the Bernardins (CB)

Favereau and Beaudoin (2015), following research carried out inside the CB, notably by Hatchuel and Segrestin, want to "think of an alternative model of the firm to the agency model and the shareholder value" (76). They find their inspiration in the German co-determination and insist in the necessity of the revolution of accounting techniques (78). They propose to reform the actual JSC by their transformation in CESO. With this change they assert that "the maximization of profit will no longer be the only one reference of the directors (administrators) and that the managers will take their decisions according to the new spirit of this mission". Instead of their classical head to head with the shareholders there will be "protected" by a new "council of the enterprise" which will be composed of representatives of the stakeholders in the CESO. These representatives will provide their opinion regarding management and report to the Board of Administrators (54–55). They also propose to "extend the representation of the salaried people inside the Board of administrators" (85): either to "the half, in the case of a high number of employees (5000), or to one third of the council for companies with more than 500 and less than 5000" (86). At last they recommend to "modify the accounting rules in order to get a non-financial conception of profit" and "to redefine social interest" (92). These proposals go in the same direction as ours. However their reference to the German co-determination seems to let the salaried people in a secondary role of management inside a supervisory board when the main decisions are taken inside the organs of direction. Moreover, their contribution chiefly concerns the question of human capital and not that one of natural capital. Here again our CARE/TDL model could offer a concretization of their wishes, with an extension to the question of ecology.

5–6 The economic bicameralism of Isabel Ferreras

In her book "Gouverner le capitalisme" (2012) this author makes a severe criticism of the past attempts to fight capitalism and shows how all of them have failed. It is the case of the Marxist experiences (based on the confiscation of private property), or the self-management ones (based on worker control) or even the Christian one (based on the idea of co-management or co-determination). She wants to propose a new concrete solution for the governance of firms so that they will no longer be in the sole hands of capitalists and, more largely, so that these firms will at last receive an economic constitution (69). She relies on the conception of the firm as an institution and wants for that to use the example of politics. Her main idea is to follow the evolution of the liberal democracies toward the bicameralism and to impose this structure of governance to firms. According to that every firm (enterprise) will be the union of, on one part, the providers of capitals and, on the other one, of the "investors of their work". These two categories of actors are indispensable and will have equal rights to the power inside the firm. The first category, on behalf of its instrumental efficiency (the economic rationality based on profit), and the second one on behalf of a political non-instrumental rationality oriented towards democratic justice (218). To achieve the equilibrium between these two forces the sociologist proposes modifying, with the help of new laws, the governance of the big firms. She will impose the creation of two different chambers with equal powers which will be obliged to find a double majority in order to find an agreement to govern the firm. The first Chamber will reunify the representatives of the different investors of (financial) capital. Symmetrically, the second one will "shelter" the representatives of the suppliers of work (110–130). The ideas which are the core of this proposal are the same as ours, notably the need for protection of the employees cannot obey an instrumental logic and that the power of financial capitalists is unjustified. However, we think that it poses the three following problems. Firstly, the ecological question, of the treatment of natural capital, is practically not treated. Secondly, we deem that the partition between the economy (the domain of the investors in (financial) capital) and the politics (the domain of the investors in work)) is not founded and potentially dangerous. It is not founded because, as we have shown, every economic choice corresponds to a philosophical, moral and political conception. It could be dangerous because, practically, it leaves to the sphere of the capitalist the task to define profit and, more largely, the rationality of "performance". All appears as if there could be only one type of instrumental economic rationality, that one of the capitalists. Due to this conception Ferreras never proposes in her book a new type of accounting although she draws the attention of the reader on this matter by quoting the works of Max Weber (159–60). Thirdly, in connection with the second remark, it seems to us that it is not possible to propose a new government of the enterprise without a new type of accounting. Notably a "constitutionalization" of the conservation of the three types of capital is necessary to replace the capitalist accounting model. Thus, as it seems, the CARE/TDL model could be a base of betterment of the valuable work of the sociologist. That said, the debate that she has introduced on the question of the bicameralism is interesting. We will resume it later in a larger context of the constitutional and legal powers at the level of the State.

5–7   The "enterprise as a common" of Swann Bommier and Cécile Renouard

In a dense book (2018) reaching a lot of questions, Bommier and Renouard dedicate one chapter to the reform of the governance of firms. They start from the theses that companies are judicial creations and always have a political dimension. They infer from that a contradiction and a problem with the mere instrumental treatment of labour capital in capitalist society. They consider that the past experiences of reform have never been in a situation to solve this problem, whether they have come from Marxist or social-democratic origins. They also deem that the German "Mitbestimmung" (English: "participation") "has not created effective contra-powers for a sustainable economic development". After this observation of general failure of the preceding proposals they find an inspiration in the writings of Ostrom to propose "a new enterprise as a common" with a "new constitution which testifies of its political character". We cannot but agree with this general view of the problem. It is however a pity that Bommier and Renouard have not prolonged their reflections by developing their proposals. However, as far as they refer to the CARE/TDL model (57) we can think that the latter could be one of the bases of their ulterior demonstration.

5–8   The participatory socialism of Thomas Piketty (2019)

In spite of some hesitations regarding terminology[1] the French economist proposes a new "participative socialism" for big companies[2] to solve today's human and ecologic crisis. He wants to "go beyond capitalism" (1117). His proposal for that is based on two main instruments: to share the power inside firms and to diffuse (disperse) the property with the help of taxation (1118–1122). For the first objective he suggests a kind of German co-management with an equal number of votes in the Board of Administration for the shareholders and the employees. He recognizes that in the

German co-determination the shareholders have the last word[3] in case of equality of votes. To increase the power of the employees he proposes to institute a limit of the right of vote for the most important shareholders and, more largely, a similar limit for any investment in capital which will represent more than 10% of the global amount of the capital (1120). To disperse the property, he suggests the recourse to the arm of taxation; he will use three kinds of progressive taxes: on property, on heritage and on revenues (1129). He insists on the fact that the philosophy of these proposals should be backed up by constitutional declarations (1145). These proposals, notably his conception of progressive taxes, head in a good direction. But, according to us, they remain unsatisfactory because they do not change the accounting system and do not fundamentally take into account the representation and the conservation of natural capital.[4] It seems to us that the use of the CARE/TDL model and of ITCH could also be a good complement to his proposals.

With this last book we have ended the review of some interesting proposals which seem to us to be compatible with our own conception of the firm. We have seen that practically all these books mention the necessity to conceive, at the higher political level, new constitutions that will foster the creation of a new type of firm. We will now explicitly state our own view of the problem.

Notes

1 Piketty recognizes that the word "socialism" is "definitely spoiled by the soviet experience (or by more recent experiences of governments which have of socialist only the name)" (1115).
2 It is no question for him to apply this participative socialism to the very small firms (1120).
3 Piketty believes that the German workers have participation in the Board of Administration, but this is not the case; in it only a participation in the Council for Supervision (Aufsichtsrat).
4 Piketty only mentions the use of the (problematic) carbon tax in matter of ecologic economics; he proposes its transformation in a progressive tax, but it remains a tax which only affects the consumers (1156–8).

6 Towards a reform of constitutions and legislative powers with ITCH

In their famous Communist Manifesto of 1848 Marx and Engels have formulated their main solutions for the realization of a new socialist economy under the control of the communist movement. They consist of three main actions: firstly, a *revolution* and taking of power by force by the proletariat. Secondly, a "despotic" attack of the right of property followed by an *expropriation* of land property. And, thirdly, the development of national fabrics in the frame of a common planning (1848, 841–842). We know what the catastrophic consequences have been of the application of these precepts in all the communist countries under the control of Lenin, Stalin and Mao Zedong. Our book will defend a totally different approach of the change of the capitalist society. An approach based on democratic decisions, the maintenance and the protection of private property, and the creation of a new type of non-capitalist market. All that in the frame of a new economic and accounting model. We will now consider the conditions of the realization of this model in today's political system. We can see today almost every day and everywhere movements of contestation of the Parliaments and the role of Parliamentarians. This is for example the case in France with the famous movement of the "*Gilets jaunes*" (Yellow vests). It appears that a larger and larger number of citizens criticize the foundations of the traditional legislative power: they consider that they are no longer represented and protected by their mandatories. The reasons for this situation are multiple. But they take their origin in five main causes. The first is that the so called "democratic" modes of pools are generally hostile to a proportional representation of the citizens. The second is that, even if the first condition is achieved, nothing guarantees that the elected persons who have competed will effectively represent them. The costs of the campaigns are generally so high that a private citizen without massive pecuniary support will have no chance to be elected; he could not rival the political forces that have these means at their disposal in the context of non-democratic processes (Cagé, 2018). The third reason is that the constitutional rules in the frame of which

DOI: 10.4324/9781003194149-9

the actions of the Parliaments are moulded do not sufficiently protect certain categories of interests. We have already shown, for example, how the decisions in matters of accounting rules, a strategic question, are generally placed under the umbrella of quasi-private committees which defend the interests of capitalists with the support of the liberal-socialist types of constitutions. The fourth is that the functioning of Parliaments occurs under the pressure of economic powers, mainly of big firms, which have at their disposal enormous monetary means to influence the decisions of Parliaments in favour of their interests, notably by the well-known means of lobbying but also, finally and even more insidiously, by the way of the media which are increasingly controlled by the allies of capitalists. To solve all these important issues it is certain that the recourse to a very large dose of proportional pools will be necessary. It also clear that it will be necessary to find more efficient ways to permit the candidature of simple citizens without the engagement of considerable amounts of money. But these actions will have their limits. Other types of questions draw our attention, notably those which concern the constitutional aspects that form the frame of the actions of Parliaments and the economic power which influences the elections.

6–1 The constitutional question

All along this comparative inquiry about the fate of the three main types of capitals, which are at the basis of any firm, we have demonstrated that, today, only the financial capital is the object of a systematic protection from the part of an international accounting law. This international law can be considered as a true worldwide constitution established by the liberal-socialists generally in power. Thus today there is a total contradiction between the beautiful principles of equality of women and men generally enounced in national constitutions and this international accounting capitalist constitution. Today's national constitutions are generally a kind of façade that mask the reality of the worldwide capitalist constitution. So, it is high time to transform the national liberal-socialist constitutions into truly democratic ones: in this sense we must finish the job of the famous French revolution which has forgotten to treat the problem of human rights *at the level of firms*. To try to put an end to this iniquitous and anti-economic situation we propose an introduction to the constitutions of all countries the two following principles. Firstly, the accounting systems of firms and nations will guarantee an equal and systematic protection of natural, human and financial capital on the basis of an accounting system of the type of the CARE/TDL model.[1] It will enunciate a basic clause of societal justice in favour of a type of new reasonable economy. It will also allow a rebuild of today's society on moral bases acceptable by all honest citizens. Some philosophers like

Mouffe, 2007, 9 and 33) refuse the perspective of a new contract of society, notably because it seems impossible to find a universal rational agreement. We believe that this an error; if the political capitalist world has been able to find a world-wide agreement on the basis of its unreasonable principles, it should be possible to find another one on the basis of reasonable principles. Thus, if we borrow the language of Ostrom, we should have a Common (constitution) for all Commoners. Secondly, equal rights of participation to the deliberations concerning management decisions in firms will be granted to the representatives of the three types of capitals. Parliaments will be summoned to vote on these two fundamental principles accompanied by severe sanctions in the case of infractions. If this kind of reform of the constitution, after a sufficient campaign of information, is democratically accepted it is clear that the actions of the parliamentarians will be fundamentally modified. They will exercise their mandate in a predetermined frame which will force them to respect the rights of the three types of "capitalists" at the basis of any economy and nation. Through this reintegration of accounting "cause" into the heart of the political structure the task of the legislators would be simplified and, more importantly, oriented towards a non-capitalist conception of society. Thanks to that passive revolution, the citizens could then develop their "communicational action", as defended by Habermas, with the considerable advantage of a precise legislative framework.[2] This leads us to the following point.

6–2   The question of the relations of power inside the economy

The inscription of the principle of equal protection of the three capitals in the international and national constitutions will not be sufficient to break today's monopolistic economic power of financial capitalism. It will only permit to go in the direction of this limitation. To achieve a real transformation of the capitalist society it will be necessary to realize, at least firstly in the big firms, a systematic and equal representation of the three capitals, meaning an ecological co-management. We have already presented its principles. But to have an even more efficient action in this domain it is also necessary to apply this type of co-management at the national and international levels in the political institutions that decide the fate of people. For that reason, we propose that, in each country, there will be a systematic bicameralism. Of course, there will remain, in a classical way, a House of Representatives of the citizens (elected with an important dose of proportionality). But this House will be seconded (doubled) by a House of the Representatives of the three types of capitals in which three groups of capital holders will have respectively an equal number of votes. This new "House of the Three

Capitals" will be obligatorily consulted on every kind of question concerning the economic, social and environmental capitals. This agreement will be necessary in order for the laws of the first House to be adopted. In France, for example, today's "Conseil Economique Social et Environnemental" should be not only maintained but reinforced in this sense. This type of democratic measure would help to prevent large companies from receiving massive subsidies without justification as a result of their lobbying capacity while smaller firms who really play the game of the ecological transition cannot receive aid because of their low capacity to make their voice heard.

6–3 A strategy for the emergence of the new economy

The experience proves that there is little to expect of today's traditional liberal and social-democratic political forces to move towards the ecological co-management that we propose. In France, for example, after a big noise about it, the recent Law "Pacte" of 2019 ends in a minimal betterment of the representation of the salaried people inside the instances of governance of firms. The liberal government has also, at least for the while, refused to follow the recommendation N°10 of the Notat-Senard report, which proposed a reform of the accounting system in a more social and ecological sense. As said by a commentator: the mountain gave birth to a mouse (Coriat, 2018). It is thus necessary to move out of this deadlock situation and to have recourse to other solutions which will permit to change more rapidly and make the necessary reforms, in the frame of democratic play. Among the instruments proposed more and more frequently by diverse social and ecological movements figure the referendum initiated by the citizens (RIC). It is probable that these mighty movements, that have understood the incapacity of the liberal and social democrats to solve their problems, will succeed one day in imposing their claim of the RICs. In that case we think that, after a large public debate, the basic principles of the CARE/TDL model, that are at the heart of a new constitution, could be voted in the frame of these RICs.[3] This will begin with a small number of (courageous) countries then extended progressively to others. Of course, today, the accounting question is considered as a secondary one but there is no reason that this will be always the case. All the more than, as we have tried to demonstrate in this book, we think that it is a vital question which is today monopolized by a small minority: the question to know *what must be conserved*. It is high time to pose it clearly in the frame of a RIC. It is time for the people of the earth to re-appropriate the politics of economics that have escaped them for centuries. Of course, in a democratic way, this referendum should offer the choice with the actual capitalist system. It will be preceded with a very large campaign of information, including the distribution of booklets emanating of diverse political forces. It will be the occasion of a public debate and a fantastic general discussion of questions up to now monopolized by so called experts, generally at the service of the capitalists and their political allies. As underlined by Coutrot (2010, 118–119) the civil society should play a fundamental role in this regard. It is often said in patronal discourses that we live in a period when the human resources and, more generally, the intangibles are the main determinants of the wealth of nations. It is time to take this assertion seriously and to give the word to the representatives of this essential capital, not in a formal way but in a practical way. Obviously the defenders of the capitalist system will say, in the name of realism, that it is impossible. They will also use the argument that the ITCH model with three kinds of partners will end in general anarchy.[4] But we live in a period full of things that have been reputed impossible in a remote or recent past notably in reason of this argument of risk of anarchy: for example, the abolition of royalty, the disappearance of slavery, the right of vote for all men and women, the co-determination in Germany a.s.o. A variant of this argument states that all those new proposals such as the CARE model are too complicated, if not impossible to apply. But the same promoters of the capitalist system defend the IFRS which are a monument of complexity with, for example, the obligation to forecast the expected cash flows of the firms over periods ranging from ten years to 20 or 30 years! As well said by Klein (2014), "this changes everything". In the light of all these elements we must not hesitate: we must be "unrealistic" to construct the future "realism" which will perhaps save the planet from its destruction, at least for the human beings! The "realists" of today who want the maintenance of the capitalist system are in fact totally unrealistic people. Of course, this proposal of an accounting RIC may take some time to be achieved. This is the reason why we propose another type of action which could be realized *immediately* by a true ecological government. This proposal relies on today's reality of accounting in big firms. Most people and politicians do not know that these firms have two main types of accountings.[5] The most well-known is the IFRS financial accounting for "consolidated accounts"; as we have seen this type of accounting is obligatory and regulated by national and international laws. But there is a second type of accounting which is not mandatory but is still present in all big groups: management accounting. It serves, as its name indicates, to manage firms and is much more evolved and flexible than financial accounting because it needs to cope with a diversity of operational tasks. We propose that this ecological government will declare that the managerial accounting must be transformed into an ecological accounting in the form of the CARE/TDL model.[6] This could be done immediately without any negotiation with other countries and, for the while, without transformation of the IFRS. This decision would be very important and useful. It will permit the public authorities to know precisely the ecological performance of these big firms and to orient the financial aids of the state toward the firms who really try to cope with the ecological crisis. Again this measure could contribute to the prevention of large companies from "swallowing" the aids for the ecological transition, notably of sovereign funds, to the detriment of the small firms that play the game of this transition. It would be also a way of informing and educating the firms, of the students and, more largely, the public. Thus, we could advance immediately towards a new ecological management without waiting for the (unavoidable) transformation of the IFRS. Another interesting possibility, proposed by Brown (2016, 141–157), would be to make *adjustments* to the IFRS' income by adding a correction for environment-sustaining costs calculated on the basis of the CARE model; this will permit to get an "environmentally sustainable residual income" to discriminate more or less sustainable investments. France could be the promoter of this accounting revolution at the global level: it has already proven in the past that its ideas are contagious ones[7]! The French revolution of 1789 has been the basis of a democratic transformation in Europe. The new French accounting revolution could be the beginning of a transformation of the capitalist economy. This leads us to a last reconsideration of the notion of capitalism.

6–4 A last return to the notions of capitalism and market

Karl Polanyi, in an outstanding book dedicated to the "great transformation" (1944/1983), describes the appearance, in the 17th century, of an economic system created and imposed by the liberal State (37–216), which has for-motive profit (85), in the frame of an "auto-regulated market" (38), which itself relies on "the freedom of contracts and private property" (211 et 268). Although he rarely uses this term[8] he obviously speaks of what he thinks to be the main characteristics of *capitalism*. He also underlines the ravages of this system which destroys social links and nature and shows that, in spite of the assertions of her (his) defenders, it has fortunately never *wholly* existed. Indeed, according to him, the self-regulation has conducted to such disasters that this system has been obliged to provide for social laws to attenuate its effects and permit its survival (217). The main target of Polanyi is visibly the market, more exactly the self-regulatory market which adjusts itself without any exterior intervention (85) by the free determination of the prices in the frame of the confrontation of the supply and the demand (86). We think that the developments that we have dedicated to the study of capitalist accounting and to its replacement by a new type of accounting permit to complete and also, in certain measure, to contest the

views defended by Polanyi. First of all, the beginnings of the modern capitalist system are well anterior to his belief: they go back to the 13th and 14th
centuries. Secondly, we have shown that there has been a constant intervention of lawyers, either those of the town-states, such as Florence, or those
of the Nation-states, who have fixed the accounting rules in matters of costs
and profit for the sake of the conservation of financial capital. Indirectly,
all these rules are at the basis of the formation of prices on markets and
permit the domination of financial capital. Hence there has never been any
free fixation of prices. Thirdly, such a destructive system has also existed in
non-market economies, notably the former soviet system. Fourthly, it may
also concern public organizations which function in the frame of a market
economy; it was the case of Renault in France before its privatization. The
type of property is thus not a decisive criteria. Fifthly, from at least the
20th century, property and contracts are increasingly under the constraints
of strict laws, notably due to accounting laws. At last, as we have demonstrated, it is possible to have a type of firm which functions with a certain
profit, without any destruction of natural and human capital. It means that
we can conceive a new concept of profit "profitable" for all. If these assertions are correct ones the criticism of the capitalist system must not concern
the existence of markets, nor the existence of a profit, nor even, private
property in general. It must concern in priority the fact that in this type of
economic system only the financial capital is systematically conserved and
gives the power, thanks notably to accounting laws imposed by politics.
This type of system is based on bad ethical principles which conduct the
firms as well as the states to bad management.[9] This is why we propose a
concrete and credible alternative, based on a new accounting system, which
permits the conservation (preservation) of the three capitals and the birth
of a new companies' law which will treat these capitals as co-managers at
equality of power in a radically new type of firm. It is not the question, as
said by Castoriadis (Encyclopaedia Universalis, 59), to suppress the "homo
computans" but to make of it *another homo computans* who respects three
capitals and not only one. The error of many critics of the capitalist economy is to have confounded the "homo-oeconomicus" with the "capitalist
homo-oeconomicus". Another error of many sociologists and ecologists is
to have confounded monetization with commodification. It is perfectly possible to conceive a new kind of normative economic theory, even based
on global monetary based markets and (reasonable) rational calculations,
which protects the eco-sphere and mankind and permits the participation of
all people at all the levels of society.

Notes

1 Rosanvallon (2020, 209–210) justly distinguishes liberal and democratic constitutions but never speaks of the of the liberal capitalist economic constitution, notably of its accounting part.

2 Clastres (1974, 20) demonstrates that it is possible to conceive and to see powers devoid of coercion. We believe that a society based on CARE/TDL ecological co-management can be a step in that direction.

3 Frémeaux (2015, 141–143) says justly that the social economy must not be imposed in the way of the "past communist promise". But why could a large democratic vote not impose this change to a minority? All the more than today this minority, thanks to its domination over the firms, imposes its accounting laws!

4 This type of argument is notably linked to the difficulty of imagining an evolution of old conceptions, notably the transformation of capitalist shareholders into "ecological and human" shareholders.

5 In fact the situation is much more complicated. These big firms have at least four different accounting systems: one for the international shareholders of the group (consolidated statements); one for the national shareholders of the subsidiaries; a third one for the tax authorities; the fourth one for the managerial tasks (management accounting). All four have different results: capitalism likes to play with the figures in function of its interests notably to boost the financial results for the shareholders and to lower these results for the taxation.

6 During certain periods of time, notably wars, some governments, particularly in France and Germany, have decided to impose specific rules even for this kind of accounting. A good example to follow!

7 Piketty (2019) also, interestingly, suggests the alliance of France with some others countries in order to change the commercial agreements. He even shows how France alone could initiate a transformation of the taxation of big international firms (1187–1188).

8 He prefers to speak of "economic society" (243) or of "market economy" (252) which, as we have demonstrated, is an error.

9 The last reporting in 2019 of the International Institute of Finance shows that the total debt of firms (without the financial sector) in proportion of the PIB is higher than that of the states (about 92% against 87%). They consider the situation as dangerous (Le Monde of the 18/10/2019 Economie et entreprise p. 12).

General conclusion

It is often deplored by the adversaries of the capitalist system that there is no concrete alternative to it, notably no alternative economic theory. We have shown that the only concrete and effective way to finish with capitalism is to replace its accounting system by another one. To this goal we have proposed the CARE/TDL model. We have begun the presentation of this model with a series of axioms which rely on a conception of what should be conserved, defining what is "capital". We hope that the reader of this book will agree that natural capital, the basis of our existence, and human capital, the basis of any economic activity, deserve to be preserved systematically just like financial capital. These axioms and their accounting consequences may be accepted, it seems to us, by those who have a secular conception of life as well as by those who prefer a religious type of life. Concerning the last point of view, we have underlined the great interest of the recommendations made by Pope Francis in his encyclical "Laudato si", which aims to modify drastically the behaviours of firms in order to give them an ecological and human purpose. If these axioms are accepted the remainder of our reasoning takes place in the field of economics. The CARE/TDL model is nothing more than the reutilization of the main tools of double entry accounting for the sake of natural and human capitals. As stated throughout this volume, this is akin to using the weapon of one's adversary against him. This model starts from the basic assumption of the big majority of economists that three capitals are indispensable for any economic activity. But we know that Aristotle distinguished two types of economies: a true economy which responds to the fundamental needs of humans and a false economy based on the accumulation of wealth for its own sake: chrematistics. Today we live in a hyper chrematistic economy based on an aberrant, dangerous and obsolete accounting system. The goal of the CARE/TDL model is to open a door to get out of it while conserving an innovative market economy, but under the constraint of the conservation (preservation) of three types of capitals. It can be considered as the vector of a "true capitalism" which will

DOI: 10.4324/9781003194149-10

replace a truncated pseudo-capitalism which has usurped and disfigured for centuries the beautiful name of capital. In a sense, to paraphrase a famous expression,[1] we have never really been capitalists! In these times of great ecological and human danger it is necessary to become "true capitalists" to protect and conserve our conditions of life. But to do that it will be necessary to dare to transform society: dare to change not only the dressing but to think radically differently. There are accountants[2] who have permitted the creation of modern capitalism. There will be perhaps other accountants who will permit its peaceful replacement with an ecological and social economy to avoid the eruption of more violent revolutions!

Notes

1 Bruno Latour has published in 1991 a book whose title is *We Have Never Been Modern.*
2 The history of these accountants and of their relationship with the economists is the object of Volume 3.

Bibliography

Abadie P. (2013). *Entreprise responsable et environnement. Recherche d'une systématisation en droits français et américain.* Bruylant. Paris.

Alvaredo F., Chancel L., Piketty T., Saez E., Zucman G. (2018). "World inequality report". Retrieved from http://wir2018. wid. world/files/download/wir2018-full-report-english. pdf.

Anker R., et al. (2011). *Measuring decent work with statistical indicators.* International Labour Organization. Geneva.

Arendt H. (1958). *The human condition.* The University of Chicago Press. Chicago and London.

Askenazy P. (2016). *Tous rentiers! Pour une autre répartition des richesses.* Odile Jacob. Economie. Paris.

Attali J. (2020). *L'économie de la vie.* Fayard. Paris.

Bachet D. (2007). *Les fondements de l'entreprise. Construireune alternative à la domination financière.* Ed de l'Atelier. Ivry sur Seine.

Bachet D. (2019). *Reconstruire l'entreprise pour émanciper le travail.* Uppr. Paris.

Bainbridge S. M. (1993)."In Defense of the Shareholder Wealth Maximization Norm:A Reply to Professor Green,50 Wash. & Lee L. Rev. 1423 (1993)

Bardy J. (2017). "Le concept comptable de passif environnemental, miroir du risque environnemental de l'entreprise". Thèse de doctoraten droit. Université Côte d'Azur.

Beaver W. H. (1989). *Financial reporting: An accounting revolution.* Pearson. London.

Berger J. (2017). *The social costs of neoliberalism-essays on the economics of K. William Kapp.* Spokeman. Nottingham.

Berger J., Forstater M. (2007). "Towards a political institutionalist economics: Kapp's social costs, Lowe's instrumental analysis and the European institutionalist approach to environmental policy". *Journal of Economic Issue*, XLI (2).

Berle A. A. (1954). *The 20th Century Capitalist Revolution.* Harcourt Brace. New York.

Berle A. A. Jr. (1959). *Power without property.* Harcourt Brace. San Diego.

Berle A. A., Means G. C. (1932). *The modern corporation and private property.* The Macmillan Company. London.

Bettelheim C. (1974). *La lutte des classes en URSS.* 1èrepériode. Maspero. Paris.

Bezard P. (2004). "Face à face entre la notion française d'intérêt social et la gouvernance d'entreprise". *Petites Affiches*, 12 (32): 45.

Blair M. (1994). *Ownership and control: Rethinking corporate governance for the twenty first century.* Brookings Institution. Washington.

Blair M., Stout L. (1999). "A team production theory of corporate law". *Virginia Law Review*, 85: 247–293.

Bommier S., Renouard C. (2018). *L'entreprise commecommun. Au-delà de la RSE.* Ed Charles Leopold Mayer. Paris.

Bonneuil C., Fressoz J. -B. (2013). *L'événement anthropocène*. Seuil. Paris.

Borrits B. (2018). *Au-delà de la propriété*. La Découverte. Paris.

Bowen H. R. (1953). *Social responsibility of the businessman*. Harper and Row. New York.

Brodier P. L. (2001). *La VAD. La ValeurAjoutéeDirecte. Une approche de la gestion fondée sur la distinction entre société et entreprise*. Addi Val. Paris.

Brown J. (2016). "Calculation of environmentally sustainable residual income (ESRI) from IFRS Financial statements: An extension of Richard(2012)". In D. Bensadon N. Praquin (Eds.), *IFRS in a global world*. Springer. Heidelberg: 141–157.

Cagé J. (2018). *Le prix de la démocratie*. Fayard. Paris.

Caillé A. (2014). *Anti-utilitarisme et paradigme du don. Pourquoi?* Le Bord de l'eau. Paris.

Capron M., Quairel F. (2016). *La responsabilité sociale de l'entreprise. Collection Repères*. La Découverte. Paris.

Carrol A. B. (1989). *Business and society*. South Western Publishing. Cincinnati.

Caroll A. B. (1991). "The pyramid of corporate social responsibility: Toward the moral management of organizational stakeholders". *Business Horizons*. July/August: 39–48.

Castoriadis C. (1975). *L'institution imaginaire de la société*. Seuil. Paris.

Castoriadis C. (1999). "Science moderne et interrogations philosophiques". In *Encyclopaedia universalis*, Vol. 17. Encyclopaedia Universalis. Paris.

Champaud C. (1962). *Le pouvoir de concentration de la société par actions*. Sirey. Paris.

Champaud C. (2011). *Manifeste pour une doctrine de l'entreprise. Sortir de la crise du financialisme*. Larcier. Paris.

Chanial P (Ed.) (2008). *La société vue du don. Manuel de société anti-utilitariste appliquée*. La Découverte. Paris.

Chenet H., Rambaud A. (2020). "How to re-conceptualise and re-integrate climate finance into society through ecological accounting?" Working paper online. Retrieved from www. chair-energy prosperity. org publications.

Christophe B., Richard J. (2018). "Deux regards écologiques sur l'encyclique Laudatosi". In Y. Levant S. Trébucq (Eds.), *Théorie comptable et sciences économiques du 15ème au 21ème siècle. Mélanges en l'honneur du Professeur JD Degos*. L'Harmattan. Paris: 299–308.

Ciriacy-Wantrup S. V. (1952). *Resource conservation: Economics and policies*. University of California Press. Berkeley.

Clark C. W. (1971). "Economically optimal policies for the utilization of biologically renewable resources". *Mathematical Biosciences*, 12: 245–260.

Clastres P. (1974). *La société contre l'Etat*. Les éditions de Minuit. Paris.

Cliff T. (1955/74). *State capitalism in Russia*. Pluto Press. London.

Comte-Sponville A. (2004). *Le capitalisme est-il moral?* Albin Michel. Paris.

Conrad J. M. (2010). *Ressource Economics* (2nd ed.). Cambridge University Press. Cambridge.

Contin R. (1975). *Le contrôle de la gestion des sociétés anonymes*. Litec. Paris.

Coriat B. (2018). *Changer l'entreprise? Quand la montagne accouche d'une souris (A propos du rapport Notat-Senard sur la réforme de l'entreprise)*. Attac. Paris.

Cornelissen C. (1913). *Théorie de la valeur*. Giard et Brière. Paris.

Corning P. (2011). *The fair society and the pursuit of social justice*. The University of Chicago Press. Chicago and London.

Costanza R., d'Arge R., de Groot R., Farberk S., Grassot M., Hannon B., Limburg K., Naeem S., O'Neill R. V., Paruelo J., Raskin R. G., Sutton P., Van den Belt M. (1997). "The value of the world's ecosystem services and natural capital". *Nature*, 387 (6630): 253–260.

Coutrot T. (2010). *Jalons pour un monde possible*. Le bord de l'eau Editions. Paris.

Coux C. de. (1832). *Essais d'économie politique. Bureaux de l'agence générale pour la défense de la liberté religieuse*. Bureaux. Paris.

Daigre J. J. (1996). "Le gouvernement de l'entreprise: feu de paille ou mouvement de fond?" *Droit et patrimoine, juillet/août*: 21.

De Lastic A. (2014). *Que valent nosvaleurs?* L'Harmattan. Paris.

Deleuze G., Guattari F. (1972). *Anti-Oedipus. Capitalism and schizophrenia*. University of Minnesota Press (2008). Minneapolis.

Delmas-Marty M. (2013). *RésisterResponsabiliserAnticiper*. Seuil. Paris.

Despax M. (1957). *L'entreprise et le droit*. LGDJ. Paris.

De Villiers, C., Rinaldi, L., Unerman J. (2014). "Integrated reporting: Insights, gaps and an agenda for future research". *Accounting, Auditing & Accountability Journal*, 27: 1042–1067.

DoddE. M. (1932). "For whom are corporate managers trustees?" *Harvard Law Review*, 45: 1145–1163.

Durand P. (1947). *La notion juridique d'entreprise. Travaux de l'Association Henri Capitant*. Dalloz. Paris.

Ekins P., Simon S. (1998). "Determining the sustainability gap: National accounting for environmental sustainability". In P. Vaze (Ed.), *UK environmental accounts: Theory, data and application*. Office for National Statistics. London: 147–167.

El Diwany T. (2003). *The problem with interest*. Copyright Tarek El Diwany. London.

Engels F. (1880). *Socialisme utopique et socialisme scientifique (Anti-Dühring)*. Editions Sociales (1948). Paris.

Etrillard C. (2015). "Contrats et éosystèmes agricoles: des mesuresagro-environnementales aux paiements pour services environnementaux". *Droit de l'environnement*, 237: 296.

Favereau O., Beaudoin R. (2015). *Penser l'entreprise. Nouvel horizon politique*. Collège des BernardinsHumanités. Paris.

Ferdinand M. (2019). *Une écologie décoloniale. Penser l'écologie depuis le monde caribéen*. Seuil. Paris.

Ferreras I. (2012). *Gouverner le capitalisme*. PUF. Paris.

Flower J. (2015). "The international integrated reporting council: A story of failure". *Critical Perspectives on Accounting*, 27: 117.

Foucart S. (2020). *Le Monde 5–6 Janvier (24): "Une catastrophe agricole commune"*.

Fraser N. (2005). *Qu'est-ce que la justice sociale?* La Découverte. Paris.

Freeman R. E. (1984). *Strategic management. A stakeholder approach.* Cambridge University Press. New Delhi (2010).

Frémeaux P. (2011). *La nouvelle alternative? Enquête sur l'économie sociale et solidaire.* Les Petits Matins. Alternatives Economiques. Paris.

Friedländer A. (1927). *Konzernrecht.* J. Bensheimer. Mannheim-Berlin-Leipzig.

Friot B. (2012). *L'enjeu du salaire.* La Dispute. Paris.

Gadrey J., Jany–Catrice F. (2012). *Les nouveaux indicateurs de richesse.* La Découverte. Paris.

Gadrey J., Lalucq A. (2015). *Faut-il donner un prix à la nature.* Les Petits Matins/ Institut Veblen. Paris.

Geiler K. (1927). *Die wirtschaftlichen Strukturwandlungen und die Reform des Aktiensrechts.* Heyman. Berlin.

Gierke O. F. (1868). *Das deutsche Genossenschaftsrecht.* Band 1. Elibron Classics. Berlin.

Giddens A. (1999). *Der dritte Weg. Die Erneuerung der sozialen Demokratie.* Suhrkamp. Frankfurt am Main.

Giraud G., Renouard C. (2017). *Le facteur 12. Pourquoi il faut plafonner les revenus.* Carnets Nord. Paris.

Gleeson-White J. (2014). *Six capitals. The revolution capitalism has to have. Or how can accountants save the planet?* Ed Aleen & Unwin. Crows Nest.

Greenfield K. (2006). *The failure of corporate law. Fundamental flaws and progressive possibilities.* The University of Chicago Press. Chicago/London.

Griffon M., Weber J. (1996). "La révolution doublementverte: économie et institutions". Séminaire international: vers une révolution doublement verte. CIRAD, 8–9/11/1995.

Habermas J. (1968). *La technique et la science comme "idéologie".* Tel Gallimard (1973). Paris.

Hadot P. (1995). *Qu'est-ce que la philosophie antique?* Folio Essais. Paris.

Hansmann H., Kraakman R. (2000). "The end of history for corporate law". *Law and Economics*, 235.

Hansmann H., Kraakman R., Squire R. (2006). "Law and the rise of the firm". *Harvard Law Review*, 119 (5) (March): 1333–1403.

Harribey J. M. (1998). *Le développement soutenable.* Economica. Poche. Paris.

Haussmann F. (1928). *VomAktienwesen und vom Aktienrecht.* Edited by J. Bensheimer. Bensheimer. Mannheim/Berlin/Leipzig.

Heidegger M. (1977). *Sein und Zeit.* Tübingen. Max Niemeyer Verlag.

Hellec F. (2015). "Revenir sur l'exemplarité de Vittel: formes et détours de l'écologisation d'un territoire agricole". *Vertigo*, 15 (1).

Helmer E. (2013). *Epicure ou l'économie du bonheur.* Le Passager clandestin. Paris.

Holling C. S. (1973). "Resilience and stability of ecological systems". *Annual Review of Ecology and Systelatics*, 4: 1–23.

Honneth A. (1992). *The struggle for recognition.* Polity Press (2005). Cambridge.

Hueting R. (1980). *New scarcity and economic growth. More welfare through less production?* North-Holland/Amsterdam. Amsterdam.

IFRS (2012). *International financial reporting standards.* IFRS Fundation Publication Department. IFRS Fundation. London.

IIRC Council (2013). *Integrated reporting*. London.

Ikerd J. (2015). *Sustainable capitalism*. Kumarian Press. Boulder.

Ionescu C. (2016). "Biodiversité et stratégie des organisations: construire des outils pour gérer des relations multiples et inter-temporelles". Thèse de Doctoraten sciences économiques. Grenoble Alpes.

Jezdimirovic M. (1974). *Teorija i tehnika knigovodstva. Savremena administracija*. Beograd.

Joas H. (1992). *Die Kreativität des Handelns*. Suhrkamp Verlag. Berlin.

Johnson C. J. (2013). "Identifying ecological thresholds for regulating human activity: Effective conservation or wishful thinking?" *Biological Conservation*, 168: 57–65.

Jonas H. (1979). *Das Prinzip Verantwortung*. Insel Verlag. Frankfurt.

Jourdain E. (2019). *Quelles normes comptables pour une société du commun?* Charles Léopold Mayer. Paris.

Jouvenel B. de (1968). *Arcadie essai sur le mieux vivre. Article "Stratégie prospective de l'économie sociale"*. Futuribles. Sedeis. Paris.

Jouzel J., Larrouturou P. (2019). *Pour éviter le chaos climatique et financier*. Odile Jacob. Paris.

Kapp W. (1950). *The social costs of private enterprise*. Ed 1971 by Schoken Books. New York.

Kapp W. (1963). *The social costs of business enterprise*. Asia Publishing House. Delhi.

Karsenty A., Sembrés T., Perrot-Maître D. (2009). *Paiements pour services environnement aux et pays du Sud: la conservation de la nature rattrapée par le développement? 3èmes journées de recherche en sciences sociales*. INRA SFER CIRAD. Montpellier.

Klein N. (2014). *This changes everything. Capitalism versus the climate*. Penguin Books. Westminster London.

Labbé J. (1883). *Note sous Sirey, 1883*, I: 357.

Latouche S. (2010). *Le pari de la décroissance*. Pluriel. Paris.

Laville J. L. (2010). *L'économie sociale et solidaire. Pratiques, théories, débats*. Points. Paris.

Lewis S. L., Maslin M. A. (2015). "Defining the anthropocene". *Nature*, 5, 19 (7542): 171–180.

Lordon F. (2019). *Vivre sans? Institutions, police, travail, argent*. La Fabrique. Paris.

Makarov B. G. (1966). *Teorija byxgalterskogo ytcheta*. Izdatelstvo "Finansi". Moskva.

Malinowski B. (1922). *Les argonautes du Pacifique occidental*. Tel Gallimard. Paris (1989).

Martin D. (2005). "L'intérêt des actionnaires se confond -il avec l'intérêt social?" In Mélanges D. Schmidt, (Ed.), *Joly*, 359.

Marx K., Engels F. (1848). Manifest der Kommunistischen Partei. In *Marx Werke Frühe Schriften* (Zweiter Band). Wissenschaftliche Buchgesellschaft(1975). Darmstadt: 813–858.

Mathey N. (2001). "L'égalité en droit privé". *Revue des Sociétés*: 359.

Mauss M. (1925). *L'année Sociologique*. Paris.

Méda D. (1999). *Qu'est-ce que la richesse?* Champs Flammarion. Paris.

Méda D. (2013). *La mystique de la croissance. Comment s'enlibérer.* Champs Flammarion. Paris.

Merlant P., Passet R., Robin J. (2003). *Sortir de l'économisme.* Ed de L'Atelier/Les Editions Ouvrières. Ivry sur Seine.

Mestre J. (1989). "L'égalité en droit privé". *Revue des Sociétés*: 339.

Moore J. W. (2017). "Introduction – anthropocene or capitalocene? Nature, history, and the crisis of capitalism". In J. W. Moore (Ed.), *Anthropocene or capitalocene? Nature, history, and the crisis of capitalism.* PM Press. Oakland: 1–11.

Mouffe C. (2007). *Über das Politische wider die kosmopolitishe Illusion.* Suhrkampf (2016 Auflage). Berlin.

Müller-Wenck R. (1972). *Ökologische Buchhaltung. Eine Einführung.* St Gallen. Mimeo.

Netter O. (1929). *Probleme des lebenden Aktienrechts.* O. Liebmann. Berlin.

Neumayer E. (1999). *Weak versus strong sustainability. Exploring the limits of two opposing paradigms.* Edward Elgar. Cheltenham.

Norton B. G. (1991). *Towards unity among environmentalists.* Oxford University Press. Oxford.

Nussbaum M. C., Sen A. (1990). *The quality of life.* Clarendon Press. Oxford.

OCDE (2011). *Payer pour la biodiversité:améliorer l'efficacité coût des paiements pour services écosystémiques.* Editions OCDE. http://dx. doi. org/10.1787/9789264090293-fr.

Ogilvie B. (2012). *L'homme jetable. Essai sur l'exterminisme et la violence extrême.* Ed Amsterdam. Amsterdam.

Ostrom E (1990). *Governing the commons: The evolution of Institutions for collective actions.* Cambridge University Press. Cambridge.

Paillusseau J. (1967). *La société anonyme technique d'organisation de l'entreprise.* Sirey. Paris.

Pape François (2015). *Lettre encyclique "Laudato si".* Parole et Silence. Les Plans sur Bex.

Passet R. (1979). *L'économique et le vivant.* Payot. Paris.

Passet R. (2003). Introduction. In P. Merlant, R. Passet, J. Robin (Eds.), *Une alternative au capitalismelibéral.* Eds de l'Atelier/Editions Ouvrières. Paris: 9–16.

Passow R. (1930). *Der Strukturwandel der Aktiengesellschaft im Lichte der Wirtschaftsenquête.* Jena Gustav Fisher. Jena.

Pearce D. (1976). "The limits of Cost Benefit analysis as a guide to environmental policy". *Kyklos*, 29: 97–112.

Pech T. (2017). *Insoumissions.* Seuil. Paris.

Percerou A. (1932). *Lois actuelles et projets récents en matière de sociétés par actions.* Thèse. Paris.

Perez R. (2003). *La gouvernance des entreprises.* LaDécouverte. Coll Repères. Paris.

Peyrelevade J. (2005). *Le capitalisme total.* Seuil. Paris.

Pigou A. C. (1932). *The Economics of welfare.* Macmillan and Co Ltd. London (1938).

Piketty T. (2019). *Capital et idéologie.* Seuil. Paris.

Platon (1993). *La République.* Tel Gallimard. Paris.

Polanyi K. (1944). *La grande transformation.* Tel Gallimard (1983). Paris.

Pottier A. (2016). *Comment les économistesréchauffent la planète. Anthropocène.* Seuil. Paris.

Rambaud A. (2015). "La valeur d'existence encomptabilité:pourquoi et comment l'entreprise peut (p)render encompte des entités environnementales pour elles-mêmes". Thèse de Doctoraten Sciences de Gestion. Université Paris-Dauphine.

Rambaud A., Richard J. (2015a). "The triple depreciation line (TDL) instead of the Triple Bottom Line (TBL): Towards a genuine integrated reporting". *Critical Perspectives on Accounting*, 33: 92–116.

Rambaud A., Richard J. (2015b). "Sustainability, finance and accounting: From the today's Fisherian- (Falsified) Hicksian perspective to a traditional accounting approach". Working Paper. Presented at the ACRN Oxford Session 10/6/2015.

Rambaud A., Richard J. (2016). "La prise en compte d'éléments environnementaux dans la mesure de la performance". 6ème Étatsgénéraux de la recherche comptable. Autorité des Normes Comptables (ANC). Paris. (French version).

Rambaud A., Richard J. (2017). "The triple depreciation line accounting model and its application to the human capital". In S. Alijani C. Karyotis (Eds.), *Finance and economy for society: Integrating sustainability*. Emerald Group Publishing. Bingley: 225–251.

Rambaud A., Richard J. (2018). "Vers une cogestion écologique fondée sur la comptabilité: le capitalo- centrisme du modèle CARE – TDL". Working Paper. Cercle des Bernardins. Paris.

Rathenau W. (1917). *VomAktienwesen: eine geschäftliche Betrachtung.* Fisher Verlag. Berlin.

Renouard C. (2013). *Ethique et entreprise. Editions de l'Atelier-Editions Ouvrières.* Ivry sur Seine.

Richard J. (1980). "Comptabilité et systèmes économiques". Thèse. Université Paris 1.

Richard J. (1983). "Comptabilité pour l'autogestion: la comptabilité des entreprises yougoslaves". In *Cahiers Français de la Documentation Française*, n°210. Paris.

Richard J. (2012a)."The victory of the Prussian dynamic accounting over the public finance and patrimonial accounting models (1838–1884): an early illustration of the appearance of the second stage of capitalist financial accounting". *Accounting Historians Journal*, 39 (1): 89–124.

Richard J. (2012b). *Comptabilité et développement durable.* Economica. Paris.

Richard J. (2013). "La nature n'a pas de prix. mais sa maintenance a un coût". *Revue Projet*, 332: 81–87.

Richard J. (2015a). "The dangerous dynamics of modern capitalism: from static to IFRS'sfuturistic accounting". *Critical Prespectives on Accounting*, 2015, n°30; 9–34.

Richard J. (2015b). *Préface à la nouvelle édition française de K. W. Kapp "les coûts sociaux de l'entreprise privée".* Les Petits Matins. Paris.

Richard J. (2016). "Refonder l'entreprise, la Société Anonyme et l'intérêt social par la comptabilité environnementale". In *Vers un nouveau cadre conceptuel pour la comptabilité internationale?* Vol. 19. Centre français de droit comparé. Paris: 175–216.

Richard J. (2017). "The need to reform the dangerous IFRS system of accounting". In R. Avi-Yonah, Y. Biondi S. Sunder (Eds.), Which accounting regulation for Europe's economy and society. *Accounting, Economics and Law: A Convivium*, 7 (2): 93–103.

Richard J., Bensadon D., Rambaud A. (2018). *Comptabilité financière*. Dunod. Paris.

Richard J., Plot E. (2014). *La gestion environnementale. Collection Repères*. La Découverte. Paris.

Richard J., Rambaud A. (2020). "Révolution comptable. Pour une entrepriseécologique et sociale". Editions de l'Atelier. Les éditions ouvrières. Ivry sur Seine.

Ripert G. (1946). *Aspects juridiques du capitalisme moderne*. LGDJ. Paris (1951).

Romano R. (2001). "Less is more: Making institutionnal investor activism a valuable mechanism of Corporate governance". *Yale Journal on Regulation*, 18: 174.

Rorty R. (1991). *Objectivity, relativism and truth*. Cambridge University Press: Cambridge.

Rosanvallon P. (2020). *Le siècle du populisme. Histoire, théorie, critique*. Seuil. Paris.

Rossignol B., Vincenti L. (2019). *Bouddhisme et capitalisme. Pour un capitalisme compassionnel*. LPM. Paris.

Rousseau S., Tchotourian Y (2009). "L'intérêt social en Droit des sociétés: regards transatlantiques". *Revue des Sociétés*: 735.

Rühle O. (1932). *La crise mondiale ou vers le capitalisme d'Etat en URSS*. Tel Gallimard. Paris.

Saez E., Zucman G. (2019). *The triumph of injustice. How the rich dodge taxes and how to make them pay*. W. W Norton and Company. New York.

Sahlins M. (1972). *Stone age economics*. Aldine. Alherton, Inc. Chicago.

Samary C. (2017). *D'un communisme décolonial à la démocratie des communs*. Editions du Croquant. Paris.

Savatier R. (1969). *Le droit comptable au service de l'homme*. Dalloz. Paris.

Scientific based targets: Sciencebasedtargets. org.

Sève J., Sève L. (2018). *Capital exit ou catastrophe. Entretiens. La Dispute*. Snédit. Paris.

Simmel G. (1918a). *Lebensanschauung*. Vier metaphysische Kapitel. Author. Munich/Leipzig.

Simmel G. (1918b). *Der Konflikt der modernen Kultur*. Verlag von Duncker & Humblot. Berlin.

Sivéry G. (2004). "La notion économique d'usure selon Saint Thomas d'Aquin". *Revue du Nord*, 356–357: 697–708.

Spash C. L. (2020). "A tale of three paradigms: Realising the revolutionary potential of ecological economics". *Ecological Economics*, 169 (March): 1–14.

Stout L. (2012). *The shareholder value myth*. BK Business Book. San Francisco.

Tchotourian Y. (2010). "Lorsque le droit nord-américain des sociétés dessine les Nouvelles frontières de l'entreprise:les clefs pour un autre futur". *Revue des Sciences de Gestion*, 243–244 (mai-août): 81.

Tchotourian Y. (2013). "Doctrine de l'entreprise et École de Rennes: présentation d'un courant de pensée au service de l'homme". In C. Champaud (dir.), *L'entreprise dans la société du 21ème siècle?* Ed. Larcier. Paris: 131–174.

Teller M. (2011). "RSE et comptabilité: pour une responsabilité environnementale, sociale et comptable". In F. G. Trebulle O. Uzan (dir.), *Responsabilité sociale des entreprises. Regards croisés droit et gestion.* Economica. Paris: 275–282.

Teyssié B. (2004). *L'intérêt de l'entreprise, aspects de droit du travail.* Dalloz. Paris: 1080.

Tönnies F. (1923). "Zweck und Mittelim sozialen Leben". In *Errinerungsgabe für Max Weber,* Vol. 1. Duncker & Humblot. Munich/Leipzig: 235–270.

Trébulle F. G. (2006a). "Entreprise et développement durable (première partie)". *JCP E,* 1257: 309.

Trébulle F. G. (2006b). "Stakeholder theory et droit des sociétés (première partie)". *BJ,* 12: 1337.

Trébulle F. G. (2007a). "Entreprise et développement durable (deuxième partie)". *JCP E,* 31: 2989.

Trébulle F. G. (2007b). "Stakeholder theory et droit des sociétés (deuxième partie)". *BJ,* 1: 7.

Ulrich P. (1977). *Die Grossunternehmung als quasi-öffentliche Institution.* C. E. Poeschel Verlag. Stuttgart.

Viveret P. (2003). In P. Merlant, R. Passet, J. Robin (Eds.), *Une alternative au capitalisme libéral.* Ivry sur Seine. Eds de l'Atelier/Editions Ouvrières: 57–62.

Walker G., Holling C. S., Carpenter S. R., et al. (2004). "Resilience, adaptability and transformability in social – ecological systems". *Ecology and Society,* 9 (2): 5.

Weber F. (2007). *Marcel Mauss. Essai sur le don nouvelle introduction.* PUF Quadrige. Paris.

Weber M. (1920a). *Die protestantische Ethik und der Geist des Kapitalismus.* Ed Jokers (2009). Tübingen.

Weber M. (1920b). *L'éthique protestante et l'esprit du capitalisme.* EdPlon (1976). Paris.

Weber M. (1921). *Wirtschaft und Gesellschaft.* Ed Zweiauseindeins. Frankfurt am Main (2008).

World Bank (2006). *Where is the wealth of nations? Measuring the capital for the 21st century.* The World Bank. Washington, DC.

Wunder S. (2005). "Payments for environmental services: Some nuts and bolts". *Cifor Occasional Paper,* 42: 26.

Zhao Y., Lou E., Ge J., Wu C. (1979[1962]). *Principles of accounting (kuai ji yuan li).* Chinese House of Financial and Economic Edition. Pekin. (杨纪琬(主编), 赵玉珉, 娄尔行, 葛家澍, 吴诚之. 会计原理(高等财经院校试用教材). 中国财政经济出版社, 1979).

Index

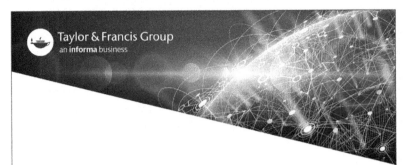